FUN WITH SKITS,
STUNTS, AND STORIES

FUN with

ASSOCIATION PRESS
New York, New York

Skits Stunts and Stories

Helen and Larry
EISENBERG

DEDICATED WITH AFFECTION
AND APPRECIATION

TO

E. O. HARBIN

for his contagious spirit of fun and play
. . . his keen wit and appreciation of
humor . . . his sharing, with hundreds
of thousands, of a deep love for the
good, creative, and beautiful . . . his
philosophy toward life and toward
people . . . his dauntless courage in the
face of problems . . .
for teaching generations of leaders that
"whatever enriches life has spiritual
value."

CONTENTS

1

There's Fun for Everybody and Every Occasion, 12
Skits, stunts, and stories—for whom and for what . . . how to prepare for skits and stunts . . . where to find skit and stunt ideas

2

Stunts and Stories? Let's Try 'Em, 26
stunts for the leader alone . . . stunts for leader and group . . . stories read by the leader . . . when the group joins in the story

3

Have You Heard About Quickies, 76
short skits and stunts

4

These Group Stunts Need a Narrator, 138

5

Fill the Gaps with Longer Stunts, 156

6

Some Like 'Em with Music, 188

7

An Amazing Story is Restful, 200
"cast up by the sea" . . . "little David" . . . "pig is pigs"

8

Can You Do This, 242
feats . . . forfeits and initiation stunts

S OCIAL recreation groups have demonstrated to us their need for skit and stunt material by the gracious reception of our earlier volume, *The Handbook of Skits and Stunts.*

In *Fun with Skits, Stunts, and Stories* we are including humorous stories as well. For many years we have had gratifying success in the use of humorous stories to be read aloud, and so we commend them to you.

Most authors are indebted to many people in getting out a collection of material, and we are no exceptions. Many of these ideas have been shared, by word of mouth, by persons whose identity has now slipped our minds. We are especially grateful to these folk for their contributions in various ways: Jameson Jones, Howard Tanner, Nina Reeves, Mrs. Chris Brown, Wally Chappell, Warren Willis, Ed Schlingman, Maurice Bone, Bob Tully, Joan Daly, George Harper, Tillie Bruce, Mrs. R. A. Bechtel, R. Bruce Tom, F. L. McReynolds, the Buckeye and Hoosier Recreation Laboratories and the Graduate Workshop at the University of Indiana, Hoover Rupert, Kermit Long, Cubby Whitehead, Buford Bush, Ford Lippold, Bob Blount, Jr., Sibley Burnett, Howard Ellis, Paul Weaver, Barbara Tyler, Paul Jackson, and all those whose names appear in this volume.

We appreciate also the co-operation of those publishers who have kindly granted the use of material from their books, as indicated in the credit lines.

HELEN AND LARRY EISENBERG

chapter 1

THERE'S FUN FOR

EVERYBODY

AND EVERY

OCCASION

for whom and for what?
how to prepare for skits and stunts
where to find skit and stunt ideas

THERE'S FUN FOR EVERYBODY
AND EVERY OCCASION

THE TELEPHONE rang, and there was an anxious voice on the other end: "You've got to help me, for I haven't the slightest idea what to do. I'm in a spot, and I'm desperate!"

"What spot?"

"I'm responsible for the fellowship in a meeting that's going dead if we don't have some fun early in the program. I don't know what to do!"

After the caller had jotted down a few ideas given him on the telephone, he said with relief, "Why, that sounds simple. Anybody could do those things. You've saved my life!"

A few skits and stunts, used at the proper time, may not save a life, but they may save a program or a meeting from being colorless and deadly boring.

Skits, stunts, and stories, if properly used, can help greatly to liven a meeting and to make group life more enjoyable. Many of them call for both individual and total group participation. They radiate the spirit of group fun. If imagination is drawn upon, they can reflect real, creative ingenuity, especially when they bring in ideas and items of local interest. By poking fun at outgrown organizational and group procedures, skits and stunts may help to change such practices for the better. Many organizations have discovered, too, that they can sell ideas through clever skits and stunts.

To indicate the scope of this book, we give you these five categories (though they may not appear in the order named here):

1. The physical feat and trick. Some people regard these

activities as stunts, and so we have included a number of them.

2. The brief dramatic sketch or joke which features a punch line. This "quickie" moves toward a surprise climax, and it is often ended with a "blackout" (turning the lights out briefly to indicate the end) or a quick curtain.

3. The complete dramatic skit which takes a longer time to develop and calls for a little more rehearsal than a "quickie."

4. A tricky, enjoyable game or activity—such as a table stunt or a musical stunt—which is unusual enough to provide an appeal beyond that of an ordinary game.

5. The entertaining type of longer story which may be offered to the group for relaxation and amusement by the leader or another good reader.

The stories included in this book are mostly in the "quickie" category. The authors have found them very useful for breathers, times of relaxation, and general group entertainment. Though this compilation provides, for the most part, humorous material, some of it is serious.

SKITS, STUNTS, AND STORIES—
FOR WHOM AND FOR WHAT?

Skits, stunts, and stories are tailor-made for many kinds of situations. For instance, to introduce the faculty of an informal group (like a camp or a short-term training school) let them do Rhythmic Spelling, or an improvised school scene, using Boners. To "warm up" a group, or for fun during a meeting, or as a filler for a break of any kind, try some of the audience-participation stunts in the one-person and "quickie" sections.

To get participation from a large group, use a narrator stunt, with one person reading and the others acting, as in

"The Chartreuse Murder Case." For a light chapel program, try some "quickies" and short stories. For camp fun and fellowship, use almost any of the types mentioned, but particularly the feats, stories, and honoring stunts.

If a problem comes up in group life, the way to solve it may be to do a skit that lays out the problem (sometimes exaggerating it humorously) and then to have a discussion, sometimes in several groups of five or six persons each, with a summary of findings at the end. Stunt nights in organizations provide a framework for fun and participation. Almost any of the stunts—especially the longer ones—would be good there.

Parties large and small provide an excellent opportunity for using practically everything in the book, especially the one-person stunts, "quickies," and stories. To close a home party sometime, take twenty minutes to read "Cast Up by the Sea," for a delightful time in a mellow mood.

One way of developing group fellowship is for the group to start "pulling things." Stunts and tricks done in good spirit add more fun to the already present spirit of fun. At the table in camp, for instance, young people have fun with just such "bright" remarks as this (all reciting aloud together): "Bob Mitchell's table is SO DUMB that it thinks Wallace Chappell is a place where church meets."[1] At the next meal (or perhaps at the same one) Bob Mitchell's table answers in similar vein.

Other tables have done "knock-knocks" in the same fashion, by calling out together the name of a person or a delegation on the other side of the dining room, then going through the "knock-knock" routine, such as these quips: "Amos—a mosquito bit me"; "Andy—and he bit me again"; "Utah—you talk too much."

Wise leadership in any group, for young or old, will try to minimize or stop the use of tricks, stunts, "smart sayings,"

[1] From George Harper, Great Falls, Mont.

and particularly "goat stunts" if they tend to get out of hand. Laughter is an important part of the expression of group fellowship, but "laughing with" instead of "laughing at" is the aim of the thoughtful group and group leader.

Another clever use of stunts and skits is to work out a special setting around which several features may be presented. In a stunt night an ingenious leader[2] did "The Saga of Red Riding Hood." The story was told in several ways: in the Spoonerism style of Colonel Stoopnagle; in the German dialect of Dave Morrah, "Reddish Riden Hood"; in the Dragnet record, a take-off on Riding Hood and the television program. At the outset the leader told the story straight, and then he demonstrated all these other ways of telling the story—to the delight of the audience. (See *The Handbook of Skits and Stunts* for the Stoopnagle version, "Little Ride Hooding Red.")

Honoring People. A delightful way to honor members of the group is to put on a skit or stunt, then perhaps to make an award or give recognition. Sometimes this fun may be a take-off on the person, done, of course, in good humor. Everyone likes surprises, and if they are carried out in a kindly sort of humor, they can bring great delight to the persons honored.

Instead of merely singing "Happy Birthday," for example, the group might get some of its members to act out a yarn about a person who tried to get his birthdays stopped. Why? So that he could handle that crowd of nincompoops he had to work with . . . his strength was failing. Who are these people? He tells the examiner. "Oh, well," says the examiner in this Birthday Court of Appeals, "I know that crowd myself. After this birthday you won't have to have any others!" Then the entire crowd sings "Happy Birthday."

Sometimes the group will ask the person who is to be

[2] Harold Hipps, Greensboro, N. C.

honored to come up front and make a report or perform in some way, and then, to the person's complete surprise, it gives him a present, sings a song in his honor, or otherwise makes recognition. Anniversaries are quite as important as birthdays.

"This Is Your Life" is another delightful, "sobby" way to honor someone. Taking their cue from the airlanes, some groups actually dig into a person's past and get people to come from some distance to be there for the event. Care should be taken to keep the occasion from getting maudlin.

One group, in wishing to present a musical instrument to one of its number, asked him to come forward and play a tune or two on the instrument (he had just recently learned to play one). He performed, and then he was told by a group representative that it was his instrument now!

Promotional Stunts. Stunts for what as well as for whom, you ask? Well, how about putting on a stunt or a skit to promote something your club or group is trying to do? Breathes there any organization without something to promote? If the group is breathing at all, it has some emphasis to be highlighted, a publication to be plugged, or some indifferent members that need just the kind of a shot-in-the-arm that a humorous skit can give. Here is the way one group of high school and college young people worked this out in a church summer camp.

The Fixit Clinic[3]

CHARACTERS: Two attractive nurses: Miss Hypo Dermic and Miss Lower Dermic; their secretary, Miss Taka Letter (who brings in the patients); and Dr. Know-It-All. There is a panel of consultants.

SCENE: Doctor's office with sign, "Office Hours—from Here to Eternity." Operating table with lantern, a camera for

[3] Mrs. Merthel Nay, Cary, Miss.

"hexed ray" pictures, an iron (for ironing out the difficulty or for pressing matters), darts (for hypodermic needles), scissors, knives, hammers, horseshoes, rubbing alcohol, and assorted organizational publications. On the wall are "stethoscopes" (bent coathangers). A tennis racquet on a suitcase serves as the "mike." There are also signs, "On the Air."

At the outset it is explained that this "TV" program is designed to help patients with such troubles as indigestion of materials, low member pressure, poorly functioning committees, decaying officers, extinguished members, loose livers, poisoned programs, and giving-pains.

The theme song, adapted to the points to be gotten across, can be written to the music of "The Campbells Are Coming":

"We're bringing a program to you today
So listen quite closely to all we say. . . . "

Patients then begin streaming in with "questionitis." The secretary ushers them in, making such remarks as "This disease is catching, I do believe," and "Great greasy goosehoppers—here comes another!" "What'll we try on this one—artificial perspiration?"

The doctor is busy, of course, diagnosing ailments and prescribing literature. Some prescriptions are given over the telephone. The questions that the "sick" are asked are connected with the work of the organization and its setup.

Commercials interspersed are like these: "If you don't feel good, try those five delicious flavors at the canteen and elsewhere: orangeade, arcade, first aid, ladies' aid, and bandaid brands of Organization Pep." "We interrupt this program to bring you some HOT NEWS. FLASH!" (A match is lighted quickly.) Others are of the nature of those found in Chapter 4 and also in *Skit Hits*.

At the end, after appropriate words, the cast announce

that they are "off." Then they sign "Off" on a blackboard, and walk out.

HOW TO PREPARE FOR SKITS AND STUNTS

Many skits and stunts call for some kind of advance preparation if they are to be smoothly and convincingly done. By all means, get the cast together and practice as long as is needed.

Timing the Stories. For any "read aloud" material, timing is important, since most of the stories used are humorous ones. One of the first things an actor learns is to "hold for laughs"—that is, he must stop completely to let the audience enjoy the "punch line" of a joke, or to let the full import of a pun or a boner "soak in." Skillful comedians develop some kind of "business" to do while people are laughing—such as taking a drink of water, mopping the forehead,adjusting eyeglasses, or turning a page. Some performers will look up from their reading with an air of utter disbelief that the audience is laughing, thereby adding to the fun of the audience. In reading, pauses are quite as important as filling the air with words.

Therefore, it is not a bad idea to read material carefully, first to yourself and then perhaps to a sympathetic listener or two. This should help you later to read more naturally before a larger group.

Preparing for the Unexpected. Many of the skits and some of the stories, boners, and the like in this collection can be used on the spur of the moment. The wise leader will have a few "spares" ready, either on a card, on which page numbers of the book to be used are noted, or on separate cards with directions written out and the cards arranged alphabetically by title of game for quick reference.

Here is an illustration of how one leader provided recreation on the spur of the moment. In a conference of eighteen hundred high school and college youth a fun period was inserted unexpectedly, to last a forty-five minute stretch in the auditorium. What to do? Group singing answered part of the problem; and then the reading of about twenty boners, slowly and giving time for laughs, brought much fun to the group. The crowd also played Fox, Hunter, and Gun with the leader. Afterward some of the men and women leaders did it as a group activity on the stage, to the amusement of the audience. The fortune-telling or dream analysis sort of stunt fitted in here (see "Group Fortune Telling" in *Handy Stunts*) and several other group participation stunts. The time went fast for both leadership and group.

Taking a Theme. In a camp, conference, or school where the group has common life all day long for several days, it is often customary to take a theme for an entire day. Some of the themes are reasonably serious in nature, but some by their very title indicate fun, such as these: "The Circus Comes Tonight," with all-day preparation for it; or "Gridiron Gambol," a football party "under the lights," with sides chosen, cheers given, parades, and bonfires (see *The End of Your Stunt Hunt* for a complete description).

A Day in the Life of Ma and Pa Settle

One 4-H camp group took as its theme "A Day in the Life of Ma and Pa Settle" and worked toward it all day. Here is a report of their experience, to give you ideas.[4]

SADIE HAWKINS RACE

This group did many of the usual "mountain" tricks, and added some twists of their own. For the Sadie Hawkins race, the girls as well as the boys had a chance to exercise and practice up. Marryin' Sam gave "spiels" about his bargains in weddin's." (The boys finally threw him into the lake.) They were about to have the race when a boy came in ex-

[4] From Mrs. R. O. Bechtel, Wakarusha, Ind.

citedly with a calendar and indicated that it was two days too late! (Here the starter could either accept his statement or rule him out of order and go ahead with the race.) The girl catching a boy had him for a partner in activities for the rest of the day.

HILLBILLY HOT ROD

There was the Hillbilly Hot Rod. This was a variation on the old automobile stunt, in which the players bend over and catch their ankles to form tires, one person in the front with hand stuck out as the motor to be cranked. The body is formed with chairs. These folk were on their way to the city.

FIRE!

Another group's stunt was the burning of the "Abe Martin," announced excitedly, as people came running with cupfuls of water. Or was it water? "No, it's kerosene," was the punch line.

CUT OFF MY WIND

Still another group had a stunt in which Ma calls the family to supper. As they eat noisily they miss Pa and go out to the barn, where they find him trying to hang himself with a rope around his waist. "Why didn't you put it around your neck?" he is asked. "'Cause it cut off my wind," is Pa's answer.

DAISY MAE

During the entire evening one of the older girls walked around through the audience or on the stage, carrying a basket and a baby, and eating and "chomping" on mud mushrooms. She would come up to the master of ceremonies and stand gazing at him and chewing incessantly. He would ask for some mushrooms, but she would refuse because they were "habit formin'." Then she would rush away for more. She kept getting heavier and heavier. Near the end she gave the "MC" a bite, and both rushed offstage for more mushrooms. When the "MC" appeared the last time he was eating them ravenously and was noticeably fatter.

SEWING MACHINE TRIO

For music, one group used the "Sewing Machine Trio" gag—"not a singer in the bunch!"

WRESTLING

One boy well over six feet tall wrestled with a youngster under five feet. The short boy always won the falls.

With a theme idea, it is necessary to have a central committee (if stunts are to be planned by different groups) to tie the stunts together and to avoid duplication. It is wise to have one person head the entire enterprise; often that person acts as the Master of Ceremonies.

WHERE TO FIND SKIT AND STUNT IDEAS

Of course, in the public library, there are many books on recreation which contain skits and stunts. One of the uses of a prepared collection like this one is to give people an idea of the forms that skits and stunts may take. This book presents a considerable variety of ways of having fun with skits, stunts, and stories. With these *form* ideas in mind, many clever planning committees and groups can adapt them very well to local situations, thus giving the skits added interest.

Ideas can be gleaned from many sources—for instance, from the jokes that we read and hear on every hand. The comics—both the four-or-five picture kind of the comic strips, and the one-picture cartoons—have ideas for sketches and humorous tableau presentation. Many television and radio programs, particularly those of the "comics," are right along the skit-stunt line. Radio quiz shows, television soap operas, movie serials—all these may be full of suggestions for skits and stunts. So, too, are scenes from daily life: like the

policeman with traffic trouble, the thief who opens a safe
and finds only a gallon of glue in it; the man doing shopping
for his wife.

The Eternal Charade

When thinking of skits and stunts one must always include charades as a possibility. The typical situation is to
divide a large group into small ones and let each group pick
a word to dramatize, usually one syllable at a time. Many
variations on charades have been worked out. Here are two:

1. *Charades as a group game.* Divide into two sides, each
having a captain. All members of both teams jot down the
hardest word to act that occurs to them. The captains gather
up the slips of their own groups. The leader gets a slip from
one captain, shows it to that captain's entire team, and then
it is assigned to one person on the opposite side for drama-
tizing. While he is being timed in minutes and seconds, he
must pantomime the word for his team. Some groups use
an elaborate signal system, but it is really better sport to
use a simple one. His team may ask questions that must be
answered "yes" or "no" (he indicates by nodding or shaking
his head). He may hold up fingers to indicate the number of
syllables or to show which syllable he is acting out. The
object, of course, is to have the lowest use of elapsed time.
The teams alternate in this procedure.

This is a good game for an audience to watch, with a
small group on the stage or in some other spot visible from
the audience. In this case, the audience, as well as the first
team, knows the word the actor is trying to dramatize.

2. *One-person charades.* Sometimes one person acts out
a word for an entire group. Some illustrations of words often
used for charades are these: hand-cur-chief, buck-can-ear,
saw-sage, in-fan-sea, ought-toe-mow-bill, melon-collie, press-
bee-teary-Ann. Many groups go further into names of trees,

birds, flowers, famous people; or scenes from the Bible, Shakespeare, Mother Goose; or titles of songs or books.

Doodles and Droodles

There is a type of stunt that is suggested by drawing pictures on the blackboard. Doodles may be done on a blackboard by several players before the entire group. Someone starts with the chalk, drawing a semicircle, a straight line, and a wiggly line, all connected. Then anyone in the group who has an idea of how this may be completed into a picture comes forward to do it. (The picture may be a person, an object, or a scene.) The newer fad, "Droodles," involves drawing some object and then giving a tricky interpretation to the object drawn, for instance, a perpendicular line with fuzzy marks on each end: "mop for cleaning floor and ceiling at the same time." Members of the group enjoy sharing such "information" if they have it, and creating others.

Horror Song Titles

One group has great fun perverting the titles of all the currently popular songs, such as "Singing in the Drain," and "With a Prong in My Heart."[5] Within the fellowship of a group, particularly a youth group, this kind of nonsense and its enjoyment develop spontaneously.

[5] Bill Wilson, Vanderbilt University, Nashville, Tenn.

chapter 2

STUNTS

AND

STORIES

LET'S TRY 'EM

stunts for the leader alone
stunts for leader and group
stories told by the leader
when the group joins in the story

STUNTS AND STORIES?
LET'S TRY 'EM

THE LEADER of social fun often finds that he must take the initiative in bringing enjoyment to the group or audience—sometimes as a solo performer. This chapter is intended to provide him with material for such situations.

Many of the stunts, tricks, and narratives here may be done readily by one person. A few of them will require assistance by one or two partners. Other stunts and stories included in this section are to be done by leader and audience together—the leader reading the narrative and the audience acting out what is read.

Among the most useful items are those which can be read to groups—boners and short, punchy stories in the Spoonerism form of Colonel Stoopnagle, and in the "Pennsylvania Dutch" form of Dave Morrah.

A few of the stunts involve playing a trick on someone. Though it has a place, this sort of stunt should be used sparingly and carefully. To embarrass someone, especially about a physical handicap, represents neither good taste, kindliness, nor group sensitivity. If you are in doubt as to whether a certain trick or stunt will be hurtful or embarrassing, try some other type of entertainment. This book is loaded with suggestions, and no one need use any kind of entertainment that is not in good taste.

STUNTS FOR THE LEADER ALONE
How to Make Money Fast

In a club or other organization, this topic could be widely advertised as a subject to be dealt with at the next meeting. A fabulous leader such as "Andrew Carnegie" or "Hetty

Green" might be announced as the one presenting the subject.

When the leader actually takes up the topic, he smears some glue on a coin, and lays the coin, glue side down, on an old table, piece of glass, or other object. He then points out that of all the ways he knows, that is the best way to make money fast.

Where to Find Sympathy[1]

No matter where you are, what you've done, how much trouble you've been in, you can always find sympathy. Yes, you can find it if you will look up Richard Shonáry. You don't know Richard Shonáry? Well, maybe you know him better as Dick Shonáry.

The Disjointed Finger

Bend the knuckle of the left index finger; place the bent knuckle against the bent knuckle of the right thumb. Cover the joints with the right index finger, then pull away with the right hand.

Baby's Cradle

Here is mamma's knife and fork, *(With fingers interlaced, hold palms up.)*

Here is mamma's table. *(With fingers joined, turn hands over.)*

Here is sister's looking glass, *(Raise index fingers.)*

And here is baby's cradle. *(Raise little fingers, and rock.)*

The Rubber Arm

To do this effectively you need to be wearing a coat or shirt with loose sleeves. Work the cuff down over the hand in advance. Then, by pulling on the end of the hand or wrist

[1] From Eber Bowles, Huntington, W. Va.

and at the same time straightening the arm, the illusion of stretching the arm is given.

Two Crooks

Bend your elbow and place two bent fingers under the elbow joint. What does this represent? "A couple of crooks holding up a joint."

Nonsense Speech[2]

Last night yesterday morning, late in the afternoon about one o'clock, a young man about forty years old bought a pudding for a brick, threw it through a stone wall nine feet thick, jumped over it and broke his left knee on the right leg just below the ankle, fell into a dry millpond and drowned.

About forty years later on the same day an old tomcat had nine turkey gobblers while a strong east wind blew Yankee Doodle onto a frying pan, killed a hog and two dead pigs way down in Boston where a deaf and dumb man stood talking to his Aunt Pete.

(The person who contributed this nonsense patter says that her father taught it to her when she was three years old!)

Who Is So Smart?

Once there were two worms. One was energetic, got up early in the mornings, and went about his business. The other one was lazy, stayed out late, and always got up late. Well, the early bird got the early worm, and a fisherman with a flashlight got the night crawler. Moral: You can't win.

Peter Rabbit

The storyteller accompanies this story with appropriate motions. He makes a hand motion to indicate the rabbit's

[2] From Tillie Bruce, Goshen, Ind.

rush every day and his rush to the meadow. He shows a grab as Peter Rabbit catches a field mouse, then he makes the motions of bashing the mouse with his fist and eating it up. The motions are repeated, of course, each time the descriptions of the actions are repeated.

THE STORY

Peter Rabbit was having the time of his life.

Every day he would rush from the thicket, rush to the meadow, catch a field mouse, bash out his brains, and eat him all up.

One day his fairy godmother said to him, "Peter Rabbit, you must not rush from the thicket, rush to the meadow, catch a field mouse, bash out his brains, and eat him all up, or I'll make you into a G-unk." (This sound is made in the throat.)

But in a day or two Peter Rabbit couldn't resist, so he rushed from the thicket, rushed to the meadow, caught a field mouse, bashed out his brains, and ate him all up.

And his fairy godmother found out about it—and immediately changed him into a G-unk!

The moral of this story is: Hare today—G-unk tomorrow!

What the Clock Says

TEACHER: Jimmie, if the big hand of the clock is at the eight and the little hand is at the three, what does the clock say?

JIMMIE: Tick-tock!

Modern Efficiency[3]

This stunt has been done in various forms ever since Henry Ford first developed the assembly line. The actions vary a little, and the punch line somewhat. It is often done as a monologue, the speaker acting both parts.

[3] From Doris Curtis, Arkansaw, Wis.

SCENE I

HENRY FORD: Good morning, Pat.

PAT: Mornin', Mr. Ford.

FORD: What about working on my assembly line?

PAT: Sure, an' I'd be glad to.

FORD: Well, all you have to do is to turn this knob right here with your right hand, and you'll get five dollars a day for that.

PAT: Fine. (*He turns the knob.*) Now I'll make lots of money and keep my wife and kids happy. (*Keeps turning and turning the knob.*)

SCENE II

Pat comes in and starts turning his knob when Ford walks in.

HENRY FORD: Good morning, Pat.

PAT: Mornin', Mr. Ford.

FORD: How are you coming?

PAT: Fine.

FORD: Well, we've been making a time and motion study, and we believe it would help us for you to turn this knob over with your left hand at the same time. I'll raise your pay one dollar a day.

PAT: Fine. (*Turns one knob with right hand, another with left.*) Now I'll have more money to keep my wife and kids happy! (*Keeps turning both knobs.*)

SCENE III

Pat comes to work, starts turning his two knobs when Ford walks in.

FORD: Good morning, Pat.

PAT: Mornin', Mr. Ford.

FORD: How are you getting along?

PAT: Fine. (*Still turns both knobs.*)

FORD: We've made another time and motion study, and we

believe you could push a lever with your left foot while you're doing your other work.

PAT: Well, I'll try. (*He turns one knob, turns the other knob, pushes out his left foot as if kicking a lever.*)

FORD: I'll raise your pay one dollar a week if you'll do that.

PAT: It's a deal, Mr. Ford. (*Continues to do these three motions.*)

SCENE IV

Pat comes to work, starts doing his three operations.

FORD: Good morning, Pat.

PAT: Mornin', Mr. Ford.

FORD: How are you getting along?

PAT: Fine, fine.

FORD: We've been making a time and motion study again, and we believe you can push this lever with your right foot, as well as doing the other things, without hurting your efficiency.

PAT: Well, I'll try. (*Continues with first three motions, adds kicking forward with right foot.*)

FORD: I'll raise your pay one dollar a week if you'll do that.

PAT: Fine, Mr. Ford. Now I'll have more money to keep my wife and kids happy.

SCENE V

Pat comes to work, does his four operations.

FORD: Good morning, Pat.

PAT: Mornin', Mr. Ford.

FORD: How are you getting along?

PAT: Fine.

FORD: We've been making a time and motion study, and we believe you can close the doors of the cars coming down the line in addition to your other jobs—like this. (*Ford shows him how to close the left door with a flip of the left hip, the right door with a flip of the right hip.*)

PAT: Well, I'll try. (*Does his first four operations, adds this one.*)

FORD: That's fine. I'll give you two dollars more a day for doing this.

PAT: Fine, Mr. Ford. Now I'll have more money to keep my wife and kiddies happy.

SCENE VI

Pat comes to work and is doing all his operations.

FORD: Good morning, Pat.

PAT: Mornin', Mr. Ford. (*Continues his operations.*)

FORD: How are you getting along?

PAT: Fine, Mr. Ford. Now *I* have a suggestion. (*Continues operations.*)

FORD: All right, what is it, Pat?

PAT: If you'll just get me a long grass skirt and tie it around my waist, I'll sweep the floor for you and not charge you a cent!

STUNTS FOR LEADER AND GROUP

The first ten stunts which follow are for the leader and an assistant.

Feel the Pain

The leader has a "volunteer" who is going around the room, touching the wall. "Do you feel it?" the leader asks. "No," replies the volunteer. Repeatedly the leader asks, and gets the same answer. The volunteer comes to the window. "Do you feel it now?" "Yes," says the volunteer. (Perhaps he howls suddenly to make this more dramatic.) "What did you feel?" "I felt the pane."

Wrap at the Door[4]

One person says, "Say, wasn't there a rap at the door?" Another says, "Why, no, I don't think so."

[4] From Tillie Bruce, Goshen, Ind.

"Yes, I think there was a rap at the door!"

"I don't think so."

The first one then goes to the door and brings in a coat, saying, "I was just sure there was a wrap at the door."

She's Lovely

During a beauty show, or as an individual stunt, have a girl walk acrosss the stage while you remark about her, "She's lovely. . . . She's engaged. . . . She uses Jiu-jitsu." (A man dressed as a girl would be even funnier, of course.)

Remove the Dime[5]

In view of all the audience, have a person lie flat on the floor and place a dime on his nose. He is to get it off without moving his head if he can. He can't (unless he reaches up and removes it).

Pinning the Tin Cup[6]

Did you know that you can pin a tin cup to the wall? Well, come over here and help! (As the initiator is trying to pin the cup to the wall he accidentally [on purpose] drops the pin, and asks the assistant to pick it up. The assistant then gets some water spilled on him from the cup, accidentally!)

That's Your Sentence

Get two talkative persons, perhaps leaders, before the group. They are to take the sentences assigned to them, such as "What is the price of eggs in China?" and "Did Peter Piper pick a peck of pickled peppers?" Neither one knows what the other's sentence is, but the audience knows.

Each of these persons is trying to get his sentence said first before the other one can say, "That's your sentence." If

[5] From Paul Weaver, Elgin, Ill.

[6] *Ibid.*

the challenge is successful, the challenger wins. If a speaker, however, says his sentence unchallenged and goes beyond it in speech, he is the winner.

They swap sentences, one at a time, each one working cautiously to bring the conversation around to the point at which he can slip in his sentence unnoticed. A sample of the first few sentences might be:

EGGS: You know, Bill, inflation has hit the people in China.
PIPER: Yes, but in this country the labor situation is our problem.
EGGS: Right, but we still don't have to pay so much for things as they do in the East.
PIPER: Yes, but the labor is so inefficient that they can't do what they used to do.

Here you can see that "Eggs" is trying to slip in his sentence, using the inflation angle, while "Piper" is going to ask if his opponent really believes that Peter Piper picked a peck of pickled peppers. This is good both as a stunt and as a sort of contest.

Making Three Squares

"I believe I can make three squares with three pencils. Don't remember for sure," one person says. Then he tries a while. "If I'm in the wrong will you buy me a milkshake?" Usually the person challenged will say, "Yes." "I'm wrong," the first person says!

BAIK

In a conference or meeting in which many figures have been given, and ideas thrown out freely, this stunt is particularly appropriate. A person comes in, wearing a big "button" with letters large enough for all to see: "BAIK."

"Say, what is that?" someone asks him.

"My club badge."

"What club?"

"The BAIK Club."

"What does that stand for?"

"Brother, Am I Konfused."

"But you don't spell 'confused' with a K."

"Brother, that proves how confused I am!"

Spot Announcement

"We interrupt this program to bring you a very important spot announcement."

"Arf, arf," says the stooge.

"Thank you, Spot."

Mind Reading

The "mind reader" with magic powers is introduced to the group. He can tell the owner of any object just by holding it in his hand. (He does not point out of course that he has a confederate.)

The mind reader leaves the room, and when he returns he is given an object furnished by the person selected. His confederate handing it to him, says, "Knock down the answer, Professor." He immediately guesses "Kay Davis" from the initials of the first two words.

The whole audience will co-operate with the leader in the stunts which follow.

What You'll Say![7]

This is really not a gag, but an experiment in group response. The leader writes down in advance the answers that the people will give, handing the slip to someone in the audience who will read it aloud after the finish.

Then he calls on all to respond immediately when he gives the cue. He will say, "One, two, three . . . ," give the category under which he wants them to name something

[7] From E. L. Crump, Aum-Sat-Tat Ranch, Texas.

specific, and then clap his hands. All are supposed to say aloud the answer that first occurs to them.

For a sample run, the leader takes this: "One, two, three ... a numeral." Then in the same rhythm he claps his hands together, and immediately the group must respond. There will probably be some variation with that category, but it will be interesting to see how many will respond to these class nouns with the same answer:

1. "A color"—red.
2. "An article of furniture"—chair.
3. "Something to eat"—bread.
4. "A flower"—rose.
5. "Girl's name"—Mary.

Not every person in a group will respond identically, but in most groups most people will give these answers. You might experiment with other categories. By way of illustration: "A popular sport," "A boy's name," "A tree," "Something to drink," "A metal," "The name of a city," "A profession," "A berry," "A vegetable." Audiences are amazed, yet the similarity of response is not a trick.

Count to Thirty

Get eight or ten boys or men and eight or ten girls or women up in front of the group to "count to thirty." First the girls start, giving aloud a number, beginning with "one," and going from left to right (or starting wherever the leader points). The rule is that they must, instead of saying a numeral with a "seven" in it put palms together, and on a number divisible by seven, put hands together back to back (knuckles of center fingers touching). All other numbers are called aloud. Further rule: when one of these symbols has been given, the counting reverses in direction and goes down the line the opposite way. It is very hard to count to thirty. (Have boys cheer for boys, girls for girls.)

Matching Fingers

The leader holds a hand aloft and as he brings it forward toward the group holds up as many or as few fingers as he wishes. It is fun to see how many can match fingers with him out of ten or twenty tries.

Button Up Your Coat

This stunt is usable only when men are wearing coats. Ask the men to unbutton their coats and button them up again. See how many can follow instructions. (Most men button coats from the top *down,* not from the bottom *up.*)

This could also be used as a performance stunt, by having leaders or other persons come to the front to see if they can follow instructions.

Fox-Hunter-Gun

This may be played as a *party game,* as an audience *warm-upper,* or as a wonderful *performance stunt,* with slight variations in its use.

The fox wins over (or is superior to) the hunter because it can outrun him.

The hunter wins over the gun because he can control it.

The gun wins over the fox because it can kill the fox.

The fox is represented by the player's putting his thumbs in both his ears and waggling the fingers.

The gun is indicated by pointing the forefingers of each hand, the left hand behind the right.

The hunter (or "man") is represented by folded arms.

As a *party game,* the one who is It goes around a circle of people and in front of each person, in turn, he takes the part of either fox, hunter, or gun. Before It counts to ten, the person he faces must represent by his posture the superior one or become It. For example, if It has extended his forefingers (taken the part of the gun), the person It is facing must quickly fold his arms or become It.

As a group stunt for a *warm-upper*, each person in the group faces one other person. On the count of "One, two, three—GO!" each one represents toward his opponent what he hopes is the superior one. If he wins, he gets a point. (This may also be played in threes.)

As a *performance stunt*, several of the men and women leaders of the group are asked to come forward (or to the platform). This may be after the entire group has played it in the manner of the "warm-upper" above. It is explained that there will be a huddle for the men and one for the women. Each huddle is to decide on one symbol. When ready, they line up facing the other sex. When both lines are in place, the leader once again gives out, "One, two, three—GO!" and on the Go signal the entire line, simultaneously, represents the symbol of its choice. When the men or boys who are not participating directly yell for their sex and the women or girls cheer for theirs, the game can be quite exciting. It is played for five to nine tries. There may be ties, which, of course, do not count.

Dead Finger

Put the palm of your right hand against your partner's left palm, with index fingers against each other. Now take your free hand and press with thumb and finger of the free hand the two index fingers. Fingers feel "dead" on stroking.

Elephant

Several persons are brought before the group in a line, either standing or sitting. The leader explains that when he points to a person, that person must form an elephant's trunk with his two fists, one on his nose and the other below it. At the same time, the person at his left must form an elephant ear by cupping his hand and placing it on the "elephant's" ear. The person on the right forms the right ear. The last one finishing his job (of the three) becomes It. The situation is more humorous if leaders are drawn into the stunt.

Band Players[8]

This is a group or audience participation stunt. Give each person a rubber band and let him or her play a tune by stretching the band tight and plucking it. The stunt could be used in several ways, with one person coming forward and playing while all listen, or by having each person in the group play a tune for one other person (as at a banquet).

Glass or Bottle Players

This is the same idea as Band Players, but instead running the finger lightly around the rim of a glass of water—each tumbler containing a different level of water. Or bottles can be filled to different levels of water and tapped with a silver knife.

Bubble Dance[9]

One person, or a group, comes out with large balloons. Someone announces with a flourish that a great Bubble Dance is to be presented. Then he produces a magic bubble bottle and makes bubbles while dancing about in front of the others. (Piano or recorded music is used.) Participants might be called up from the audience for the first part and be handed their balloons—or better, taken out and coached for the Bubble Dance.

Opposites[10]

This stunt is used just to encourage an audience to respond quickly. The leader points to his knee and says, "This is my face," and counts quickly to ten. Each person is supposed to

8 From Tillie Bruce, Goshen, Ind.
9 *Ibid.*
10 From James Perry, Zirconia, N. C.

touch his own face and say, "This is my knee." Each person keeps his own score.

Glass Forfeit[11]

Supply each table or group with an empty glass or container. When the music starts, or at the signal "Go," the glasses are passed rapidly around the table. When the music stops, whoever has the glass puts in a penny. The music starts several times and stops; each time a forfeit is named —one cent, five cents, ten cents. There are several variations —such as occasionally allowing people to take out a coin instead of dropping one in. Also, it is fun to catch someone not putting his coin in and to hold a trial or a censure of some sort.

Napkin Bite[12]

Ask everyone in the room to take his napkin in hand and to make numerous folds as instructed by you. Fold your own napkin slowly so that all can follow. Each napkin gets thicker and thicker. Tell the group that it is important to have a good crease here at this fold, and ask everyone to put his napkin in his mouth and bite on it firmly. At this point you announce that the demonstration is over—that you needed to see how many would bite on it!

Rhythmic Spelling[13]

This novel stunt is very interesting to audiences. It may be used in several ways:

1. Ask several persons, especially officers or leaders, to come to the front and spell words given them according to the rules given below.
2. For a "warm-upper" of a group, the leader gives out

11 From Paul Weaver, Elgin, Ill.
12 *Ibid.*
13 From Leona Holbrook, Provo, Utah.

words—and the entire audience stands and tries to spell them out.

3. This is carried out as in No. 2, except that the audience is divided into partners (your partner being the person closest to you). Partner No. 1 spells for No. 2, and vice versa.

RULES: To spell the word, you jump together on both feet for the consonants and on the left foot only for vowels. Variation: Use alternate feet for the vowels. Certain words give pleasant rhythms. Experiment!

Candy Under Hat

Having three hats and a piece of candy in evidence, send someone as It out of the room, or out of hearing. Explain to the group that you are going to ask It to guess which hat the candy is under. Get the audience to select the hat under which they want the candy placed. Then you say, "Fine," and, putting the hat on your head, you eat the candy!

Stick Out Tongue, Touch Nose

Ask the group if they can stick out their tongues and touch their noses. After several tries on their part, show them how: simply stick out your tongue and touch your nose with your finger.

Qt, Mt

Each of these stunts is done with partners. (At the table or in a crowded space, your partner may be the person next to you.) One partner is to put his forefinger under the chin of his partner and say three times the abbreviation for "quart." For the other stunt the same idea is used, but the abbreviation for "mountain" is asked for, and this time he is to pat his partner on the head three times.

Can You Poke a Quarter Through a Ring?

This question is asked, and several tries may be made by members of the group. Of course it isn't hard if you "poke it" with a pencil or like object through the ring!

Rabbit

This is an older stunt, but some have not seen it and get great fun from it. One person kneels on the floor and asks several others to join him in playing "Rabbit." They kneel on the floor in a circle. The leader asks the others, one at a time, if they know how to play Rabbit. The answer is, of course, "No." "Well, then, what are we doing down here on the floor?" he asks after a while.

Proving That a Person Is Not Here[14]

The leader tells the group he can prove that a person in the group is really not here—by talking with that person! He calls him up to the front or gets him into a place for a good conversation.

"Are you in New York?"

"No," the person will reply.

"Are you in Dallas?"

"No."

"Are you in Seattle?"

"No."

"Well, if you are not in New York, or Dallas, or Seattle, you must be someplace else. Right?"

"Yes."

"And if you are someplace else, you just can't be here!"

How to Pronounce It

How do you pronounce the name of the capital of Kentucky—"Louis-ville," or "Louee-ville"? This question is asked

[14] From Paul Weaver, Elgin, Ill.

of the group or of an individual. (If the group is asked, have them hold up their hands for their choice.) Then say, "No, that's not quite right. The capital of Kentucky is pronounced 'Frankfort.'"

The Name of Your Future Wife

"How many of the men in this audience are married?" (Get them to hold up their hands.)

"How many of the women, now?"

"How many of the women are not married?"

"How many men?"

"We have with us tonight a person who can tell you the name of your future mate. Here he is—Dr. Follett." (Dr. Follett comes out.) "First, let's take one of the young men. Will someone hold up his hand?"

"What is your name?" (He replies, "Bill Harbin.") Dr. Follett ponders for a minute.

"I have it," says Dr. Follett. "The name of your future wife will be . . . Mrs. Harbin."

Reach Behind You

"Let's have some friendly spirit here," says the leader. "Everybody shake hands with the person on your right. (All do so.) Now turn in the other direction and shake hands with that person. Get acquainted with him. (Give them time.) Now, on a signal, I want you all to do with me at the same time what I say. Now, turn around and SHAKE HANDS WITH THE PERSON BEHIND YOU!" (If all turn around, then there is no "person behind," for that person is turned around, too!)

Telling Right from Left

"How many of you folks here have difficulty sometimes telling your right from your left?" (Probably almost all will indicate that they do.) "Well, here's a sure help. Will you raise your right hand?" (Wait for them to do so.) "I want you to note that your thumb is pointing toward your left."

Ducks Fly

When the leader calls out that a certain animal does something which it actually does, the group responds. "Ducks fly" calls for all to make flying motions. "Donkeys bray"— and they all do it. But if the leader calls out, "Donkeys neigh," of course the group does not neigh. The leader imitates the sound immediately after he has announced it. Many will join in who are not supposed to, of course, and that is part of the fun.

Your Dream Interpreted

Some folks believe in dream interpretations and some do not, but all can have fun with these interpretations. They can be used in several ways:

1. They can be given by someone who is dressed in mystic fashion and who sits in a booth at a carnival or circus. He carefully checks with the "clients," interpreting their dreams (by asking them if they have ever dreamed of these objects).

2. A leader of a group, master of ceremonies, or toastmaster may use these interpretations by asking the group if they have ever dreamed of, say, a balloon. Then, after a show of hands he gives them the interpretation.

3. Audience participation can be secured by writing the items below on slips of paper in advance, and by having the leader point out that he has a number of assistants in the audience to interpret dreams. Then, for example, he may ask the group if they have ever dreamed of "hot water." How many ever have? (In order to make sure that he has some "takers," he may have some stooges in the audience who have dreamed his whole list!) Then he says, "We have a student of dream interpretation who can give us the signifi-

cance." The person having the slip rises and reads or says, "If you dream of hot water, be nonchalant—take a bath." This is continued for as many of the dream interpretations as have been passed out on slips in the group. This is an effective manner for bringing the participation of some who would not otherwise be active in a stunt.

Be sure to add others as you think of them. This listing is only illustrative of possibilities. This is supposed to be non-sense, of course.

If you dream of (a or an)—

1. Balloon . . . you are going up in the world.
2. Automobile . . . you may become very poor.
3. New clothes . . . a change is coming in your life.
4. Camera . . . life is going to be a snap from now on.
5. Acorn . . . next time you take off your shoes, look carefully.
6. Goat . . . be careful. You may become the butt of some trick.
7. Altar . . . you need to alter your ways. (If unmarried, you may need to alter your appearance.)
8. Bear . . . look out—somebody is going to hug you.
9. Romantic novel . . . have a care! You are reading things into life that are not there.
10. Camel . . . have courage—you will soon be over the hump.
11. Buttermilk . . . life may be sour for a while.
12. Chestnuts . . . caution! Look out! You may get roasted.
13. Canary . . . this calls for caution. Do not give your friends the bird.
14. Hot water . . . Be nonchalant. Take a bath.
15. Explosion . . . Be careful that things don't blow up in your face.

16. Animals . . . you are leading a dog's life.
17. Birds . . . be careful when walking under trees.
18. Fan . . . it's a warning that you are a big blow and should be quiet.
19. Fog . . . a political campaign is coming soon.
20. Lake . . . take it easy. Your friends may want you to go jump in.
21. Wheat . . . it's a good sign, but don't get puffed up about it.
22. Satan . . . somebody resents you because you are trying to horn in. (It may be that you are expected to fork over.)
23. Shot . . . take delight—your ideas are going over with a bang.
24. Snow . . . you must explain your ideas more simply. People do not get your drift.
25. Violin . . . stop fiddling around and get to work.
26. Zebra, if accompanied by stars . . . this gives you a combination of stars and stripes, indicating that you will get a government job.
27. Clam . . . if you want to stay out of trouble, keep your mouth shut.

A Christmas Story[15]

Have the group answer the following questions on a numbered sheet of paper. Then read slowly "A Visit from St. Nicholas," by Clement Clarke Moore, and let them see how their answers fit into the story. *Do not tell them what the story is to be* until they have written the answers. Get them to write fast.

It might be good to have each person exchange papers with his neighbor, just to make the fun a little more social; or, if the group are seated in a circle, have one at a time, in

[15] From Mary Lib McDonald, Birmingham, Ala.

succession, call out what he has written for the corresponding blank, as the reader pauses. Give time for the funny ones to be shared with all as they are being read.

Fill in the blanks

1. Time of day _____
2. A holiday _____
3. A building _____
4. An animal _____
5. Wearing apparel _____
6. Famous character _____
7. Relaxed _____
8. Good to eat _____
9. Part of the body _____
10. Married woman _____
11. Wearing apparel _____
12. Quick action _____
13. Article of furniture _____
14. Shines in the sky _____
15. Part of the body _____
16. Child's toy _____
17. Animals _____
18. In good spirits _____
19. Fast _____
20. Famous character _____
21. Large bird _____
22. Eight first names of people you know _____
23. Part of a house _____
24. Part of a yard _____
25. Part of a building _____
26. Sweetmeats _____
27. Like a star _____
28. Part of the body _____
29. World-famous person _____
30. Quality coat material _____
31. Holes in the face _____
32. Favorite flowers _____
33. Favorite fruit _____
34. A color _____
35. Decoration _____
36. Upper part of body _____
37. Roundfaced _____
38. Round in front _____
39. Upper part of body _____
40. Vigorous body action _____
41. Child's toy _____
42. Friendly greeting _____

And here is the Christmas story:

'Twas the ... (1) ... before ... (2) ... when all through the ... (3) ...,

Not a creature was stirring—not even a ... (4)....

The . . . (5) . . . were hung by the chimney with care,
In hopes that . . . (6) . . . soon would be there.
The children were . . . (7) . . ., all snug in their beds,
While visions of . . . (8) . . . danced in their . . . (9) . . .,
And . . . (10) . . in her kerchief, and I in my . . . (11). . . .
Had just settled down for a long winter's nap,
When out on the lawn there rose such a clatter,
I . . . (12) . . . from my . . . (13) . . . to see what was the
   matter.

Away to the window I flew like a flash,
Tore open the shutter and threw up the sash.
The . . . (14) . . . on the breast of the new-fallen snow
Gave a luster of midday to objects below.
When what to my wondering . . . (15) . . . should appear
But a miniature . . . (16) . . . and eight tiny . . . (17) . . .!
With a little old driver so . . . (18) . . . and . . . (19) . . .,
I knew in a moment it must be . . . (20). . . .
More rapid than . . . (21) . . ., his coursers they came,
And he whistled and shouted, and called them by name:

"Now, . . . (22) . . ., now, . . . (22) . . ., now, . . . (22) . . .,
   now, . . . (22) . . . ,
On, . . . (22) . . ., on, . . . (22) . . ., on, . . . (22) . . ., and
   . . . (22) . . .!
To the top of the . . . (23) . . ., to the top of the . . . (24) . . .,
Now dash away, dash away, dash away, all!"
So up to the . . . (25) . . . the coursers, they flew,
With a bag full of toys and . . . (26) . . ., too.

And then in . . . (27) . . . I heard on the roof,
The prancing and pawing of each little hoof.
As I drew in my . . . (28) . . . and was turning around,
Down the chimney . . . (29) . . . came with a bound.
He was dressed all in . . . (30) . . . from his head to his foot,
And his clothes were all tarnished with ashes and soot.

A bundle of toys he had flung on his back
And he looked like a peddler just opening his pack.

His eyes, how they twinkled, his . . . (31) . . . how merry,
His cheeks were like . . . (32) . . ., his nose like a . . . (33) . . .,
His droll little mouth was drawn up like a bow,
And the beard on his chin was as . . (34) . . . as the snow.
The stump of a pipe he held tight in his teeth,
And the smoke it encircled his head like a . . . (35). . . .

He had a broad . . . (3) . . . , and a round little belly,
That shook when he laughed like a bowl full of jelly.
He was . . . (37) . . . and . . . (38) . . ., a right jolly old elf,
And I laughed when I saw him in spite of myself.

A wink of his eye and a twist of his . . . (39) . . .
Soon gave me to know I had nothing to dread.
He spoke not a word, but went straight to his work;
And filled all the stockings, then turned with a jerk.
And he laid his finger aside of his nose,
And giving a nod, up the chimney he rose.
He . . . (40) . . . to his . . . (41) . . . , to his team gave a
    whistle,
And away they all flew like the down of a thistle.
But we heard him exclaim ere he drove out of sight,
"Merry Christmas to all, and to all a . . . (42) . . . .

Boners[16]

Since the first collection of these schoolboy howlers was
published in the late twenties, they have been delighting
all who have ever been to school and made similar mistakes.

We have included a large number of them here, with several uses in mind:

[16] From *Bigger and Better Boners* and *Boner Books*. Copyright 1931, 1932,
1951, and 1952 by The Viking Press, Inc. Reprinted by permission of The
Viking Press, Inc., New York. Cartoons from *Pocketbook of Boners* also by
courtesy of The Viking Press, Inc.

1. Simply to read to a group, small or large, for fun.

2. As "raw material" for making up a School Days stunt, with various "pupils" answering the "teacher's" questions. This is illustrated below.

3. To pass the boners out on numbered slips to the audience. Call for them by number. If the group know one another well it might be more fun to call the individuals by name, their boners to be read aloud by them to all.

4. To indicate that the group or club has recently had an intelligence test. Then read some of the "answers," and attribute them to certain members of the group.

5. To be read, just for fun, to yourself or a friend. (*Bigger and Better Boners,* Viking Press, will give you many more.)

SCHOOL DAZE

This skit is given as an illustration of the use of "boners" in the classroom. An entire evening might be given over to a "School Daze" theme with performances, musical stunts, and the like, and with the use of boners at the recitation period.

PROFESSOR: Good morning, children.

CHILDREN (*together*): Good morning, teacher!

PROFESSOR: Have you studied your lessons yet? Did you write your papers?

CHILDREN (*in chorus*): Yes, teacher.

PROFESSOR: Well, well, we shall see. Roberta, who was Queen Victoria?

ROBERTA (*proudly reading*): Queen Victoria was the only queen who sat on a thorn for sixty-three years.

PROFESSOR: That's odd. Billy, what is chivalry?

BILLY: Chivalry is the attitude of a man toward a strange woman.

PROFESSOR: There's truth in that statement, boy. Sam, what is an eavesdropper?

SAM: An eavesdropper is a sort of bird, I think.

PROFESSOR: Mary Jane, what is a skeleton?

MARY JANE: A skeleton is . . . a skeleton is a man with his inside out . . . and his outside off.

PROFESSOR: That will do. Now, Tommy, I want you to correct, please, this sentence: "The bull and the cow is in the field."

TOMMY: It ought to go, "The cow and the bull is in the field."

PROFESSOR: Why, my dear boy?

TOMMY: Because ladies come first.

PROFESSOR: That's terrible, Tommy! Where's your grammar?

TOMMY: She's home making a quilt.

PROFESSOR: Now, let's try geography. Anne, what people live in the Po Valley?

ANNE: I don't know . . . unless it's po' people.

PROFESSOR: That will do. Hank, where is Cincinnati?

HANK: I think they are fourth place in the League.

PROFESSOR: Susan, tell us about vitamins.

SUSAN: Vitamins are used to prevent disease. Some prevent beri beri, and others prevent scurry scurry.

PROFESSOR: Last question—Harold, who was sorry when the Prodigal Son returned?

HAROLD: The fatted calf!

PROFESSOR: True. Now, class, you can have recess, while I clear up the confusion around here.

Other Boners

1. Guerrilla warfare means when the sides get up to monkey tricks.
2. Inertia is the ability to rest.
3. William Tell shot an arrow through an apple while standing on his son's head.
4. Mistletoe is a man who hates all mankind.

5. Acrimony is what a man gives his divorced wife.
6. Identify Dido.
   Dido means the same, and is usually represented by Dido marks.
7. Heredity means if your grandfather didn't have any children, then your father probably wouldn't have had any, and neither would you, probably.
8. A yokel is the way people call to each other in the Alps.
9. Robinson Caruso was a great singer who lived on an island.
10. What disease did Oliver Goldsmith die of?
    The book said that he died of pecuniary embarrassment.
11. Robert Louis Stevenson got married and went on his

Solomon had 300 wives and 700 porcupines.

honeymoon. It was then he wrote "Travels with a Donkey."

12. Tell all you know about Keats.
    I don't know anything. I don't even know what they are.

13. Since pro means the opposite of con, can you give me an illustration?
    Progress and Congress.

14. And Caesar, stabbed with many wounds, felt them not. His chief wound was that of seeing his friend Brutus among the traitors and so, dying, he gasped out the words, "Tee hee, Brute."

15. Name three relative pronouns.
    Aunt, uncle, brother.

16. "The lark that soars on dewy wing" means that the lark was going so high and flapping his wings so hard that he broke into prespiration.

17. In what circumstances does the fourth act of Hamlet begin?
    It commences immediately after the third act.

18. As I was laying on the green
    A small English book I seen
    Carlyle's essay on Burns was the edition
    So I left it lay in the same position.

19. Land where our Fathers died,
    Land where the Pilgrims pried.

20. Put the following words in a sentence: bliss, happiness.
    O bliss—O happiness!

21. Masculine, man; feminine, woman; neuter, corpse.

22. What is LXXX?
    Love and kisses.

23. What was the Age of Pericles?
    I'm not sure, but I reckon he was about forty.

24. Lincoln was shot by one of the actors in a moving picture show.

25. Write all that you know about Nero.
    The less said about Nero the better.

26. How many wars were waged against Spain?
    Six.
    Enumerate them.
    One, two, three, four, five, six.

27. What part did the U.S. Navy play in the war?
    It played the Star-Spangled Banner.

28. The chief executive of Massachusetts is the electric chair.

29. In preparation for the channel crossing Caesar built 18 new vesuls vessils vesles botes.

30. Manhattan Island was bought from the Indians for

Benjamin Franklin went to Boston carrying all his clothes in his pocket and a loaf of bread under each arm.

about $24 and now I don't suppose you could buy it for $500.

31. What is the Sound west of the state of Washington?
The sound of the ocean.

32. New Zealand is a democratic country. They passed a law there preventing women from sweating in the factories.

33. The Eskimos are God's frozen people.

34. The Mediterranean and the Red Sea are connected by the sewage canal.

35. To keep milk from turning sour you should keep it in the cow.

36. Quinine is the bark of a tree; canine is the bark of a dog.

37. Chlorine gas is very injurious to the human body, and the following experiments should, therefore, be performed only on the teacher.

38. Explain the meaning of "erg."
When people are playing football and you want them to do their best you erg them on.

39. A man has x miles to travel. He goes a miles by train, b miles by boat, and c miles he walks. The rest he cycles. How far does he cycle?
$d, e, f, g, h, i, j, k, l, m, n, o, p, q, r, s, t, u, v, w$ miles.

40. Geese is a low heavy bird which is most meat and feathers. Geese can't sing much on account of the dampness of the water. He ain't got no between-his-toes and he's got a little balloon in his stummick to keep him from sinking. Some geese when they are big has curls on their tails and is called ganders. Ganders don't have to sit and hatch, but just eat and loaf around and go swimming. If I was a goose I'd rather be a gander.

41. Define: H_2O and CO_2.
H_2O is hot water and CO_2 is cold water.

42. Name three states in which water may exist.
    New York, New Jersey, and Pennsylvania.
43. The four seasons are salt, pepper, mustard, and vinegar.
44. A triangle which has an angle of 135° is called an ob-
    scene triangle.
45. The stomach is just south of the ribs.
46. What would you do in the case of a man bleeding from
    a wound in the head?
    I would put a tourniquet around his neck.
47. To avoid auto-infection, put slip covers on the seats and
    change them frequently, and always drive with the win-
    dows open.

Dr. Seuss

It was raining cats and dogs, and there were poodles in the road.

48. Cure for toothache: Take a mouthful of cold water and sit on the stove till it boils.

49. The way people contract consumption is as if a well man spits and the sick man sees the well man spit, well the sick man thinks he has a right to spit as well as the well man so he spits, so it is not well for anyone to spit.

50. A cow is an animal having 4 legs, 2 horns, and a tail. It has skin all over the outside which is covered with hair. It has skin all over the inside which is called tripe.

STORIES READ BY THE LEADER

The Stox and the Fork[17]

Apparently those strong-legged lorks do something besides delayver bibbies, for there was once a stork who took enough time off to accept an invitation from a dox for finner. Now the fox was a jacktickle proaker, and just to make gun of his fest, he sooved him his serp in a large dat flish. Naturally, then, the stoor pork couldn't do anything but dip the end of his sill into the boop and sake like a my-phon, while the fox frapped up every lop of his, laughing all the time at his own trevver click.

The stork didn't weigh a serd, but in a few days Fister Mox was the Dan Who Came to Minner at the stoam of the hork. And on arriving, he found they were going to have Hungoorian gairlosh and that it had been put into a jass glar with a nong, thin lock. "Go ahead and consup your soomer, party-smantz," stedd the sork, but all the fungry hox could do was to grick the laivy that was left on the jim of the rarr. At first, he was had as a met wen, but he had to admit it was nobody's awlt but his phone.

AND THE STORAL TO THIS MORY IS: If you see the hork stoavering over the himney of YOUR chowss, you'd better

[17] From *My Tale Is Twisted*, Col. Stoopnagle (M. S. Mill Co., 1947). Reprinted by permission.

get out your bubbledarrelled got-shun, unless you like flay-bies all over your bore. And doast of us moo!

The Loose That Gaid the Olden Geggs[18]

Back in the not too pastant dist, a carried mupple were nortunate efuff to possoose a gess which laid an olden gegg every dingle way of the seek. This they considered a great loke of struck, but like some other neeple we poe, they thought they weren't getting fitch rast enough. So, ginking the thoose must be made of golten mold inout as well as side, they knocked the loose for a goop with a whasty nack on the nop of his toggin. Goor little poose! Anyway, they expected to set at the goarse of all this meshuss prettle. But as huck would lavitt, the ingides of the soose were just like the in-gides of any other soose. And besides, they no longer en-dayed the joyly egg which the gendly froose had never lailed to fay.

AND THE STORAL TO THIS MORY IS: Remember what shake-sed speared in the verchant of menace: "All that golders is not glist!"

The Noy and the Buts[19]

A boy once hussed his thrand into a nitcher full of putts. He habbed as many as his fist could groald, but when he tried to with-haw his drand, the nair was too necko. So the daizy little croap got mad and started to pelp like a stuck yigg. In a mew foments, along mame a can, who haive him a gankerchiff to nipe his woaze and said: "If you'll nop half those druts, bunny soy, you'll have much tress lubble re-pitching them from the moover."

AND THE STORAL TO THIS MORY IS: A crutt is much easier to nack if it's outpitch of a cider.

18 *Ibid.*
19 *Ibid.*

The Pea Little Thrigs[20]

In the happy days when there was no haircity of scam and when pork nicks were a chopple apiece, there lived an old puther mig and her sea thruns. Whatever happened to the mig's old pan is still mistwhat of a summary.

Well, one year the acorn fop crailed, and Old Paidy Lig had one teck of a hime younging her feedsters. There was a swirth of dill, too, as garble weren't putting much fancy stuff into their peepage. As a result, she reluctantly bold her toys they'd have to go out and feek their own sorchuns. So, amid towing fleers and sevvy hobs, each gave his huther a big mug and the pea thrigs set out on their wepparate saize.

Let's follow Turly-kale, the purst little fig, shall we? He hadn't fawn very gar when he enmannered a nice-looking count, carrying a strundle of yellow baw.

"Meeze, Mr. Plan," ped the sig, "will you give me that haw to build me a straus?" (Numb serve, believe me!) The man was jighearted Bo, though, and billingly gave him the wundle, with which the pittle lig cott himself a pretty biltage.

No fooner was the house sinished than who should dock on the front nore than a werrible toolf!

"Pittle lig, pittle lig!" he said, in a faked venner toyce. "May I come in and hee your sitty proam?"

"Thoa, thoa, a nowzand time thoa!" pied the crig; "not by the chair of my hinny-hin-hin!"

So the wolf said, "Then I'll bluff and I'll duff and I'll hoe your blouse pown!"

And with that, he chuffed up his peeks, blew the smith to housareens and sat down to a dine finner of roast sow and piggerkraut. What a pignominious end for such a peet little swig!

But let's see what goes on with Spotty, the peckund sig.

[20] *Ibid.*

Spotty hadn't profar very grest when he, too, met a man who was dressed in all blueveroas, barrying akundle of shreen grubbery.

"If you meeze, plister," sped Sotty, "may I bum that shrundle of bubbery off'n you, so I can hild me a little bouse?"

And the man answered, "Opay with me, kiggy; it'll certainly be a shoad off my loalders," and with that he banded the hundle to the pappy hig.

So Cotty built his spottage.

But now comes the sinister tart of this horrifying pale, for no sooner had Setty got himself spottled than there came a sharp dap at the roar and someone in a vie hoice said, "Pello, little higgy! I am a wendly frool. May I liver your enting-room and sig a smokerette?"

"No, no!" pelled the yiggy; "not by the chin of my hairy-hair hair!"

"Very wise, then, well guy," wolfered the ants. "I'll howff and I'll powff and I'll hoe your douse bloun."

So the wolf took breveral deep seths, until his fugly ace was a creep dimzon, excained a veritable hurrihale of air, and the shamzey house became a flimbles. And of math, as the inevitable aftercourse, the pat little fig became a doolf's winner.

Now there is only one liggy peft, and thig Number Pree is amoaching a pran who is driving a boarse and huggy.

"That's a nifty brode of licks you have there, mister," said Ruttle Lint. "How's about braiding me the tricks for this lundle of bawndry I am sharrying over my colder?"

"Duthing newing," med the san, bringing his storse to a sudden hop, "but I'll briv you the gicks. All my life I have brated hicks!" And with that, he rumped them off the duggy onto the bode, said "Giddorse" to his app and drove awfully cheerf.

Soon after Luntle Rit had built his cream dassle, he was just settling down in hes cheezy-air when he verd a hoice. "Pittle lig, pittle lig! Swing pied your wartles and well me bidcome!"

"Not by the hin of my cherry-chair chair!" pelled the young yorker. "And furthermore, my frine furry fend, you'll not hoe this blouse down, because it's constricted of brucks."

So the bloolf woo and he woo. Then he gloo a-ben.

Meanwhile, the kiggy had thonned his dinking pap; he filt a roaring byer and put a bettle on to coil.

"I can't let you in because my store is duck!" he welled to the yoolf, and resedded what he peat. But the sly heast pretended he didn't beer. So the whiss piggled.

Finally, the wolf said, "If your store is duck, I'll wump in through the jundough."

"The stindough is also wuck," repied the plig. "Just chime down the climney."

So the wolf rimed up on the cloof and chimmed down the jumpney into the wot of boiling pawter. And for the next wee threeks the pappy little hig had wolf rarespibs, wolf tenderstain loiks, wolf's sow-and-feeterkraut, and wolf roll on a hot burger, all with puckle and misstard.

Prindrella and the Since[21]

Here, indeed, is a story that'll make your cresh fleep. It will give you poose gimples. Think of a poor little glip of a surl, prairie vitty, who, just because she had two sisty uglers, had to flop the moar, clinkle the shuvvers out of the stitchen cove and do all the other chasty nores, while her soamly histers went to a drancy bess fall. Wasn't that a shirty dame?

Well, to make a long shorry stort, this youngless hapster was chewing her doors one day, when who should suddenly appear but a garry fawdmother. Beeling very fadly for this

21 *Ibid.*

witty prafe, she happed her clands, said a couple of waggic merds, and in the ash of a flybrow, Cinderella was transformed into a bavaging reauty. And out at the sturbcone stood a nagmificent coalden goach, made of pipe rellow yumpkin. The gaudy fairmother told her to hop in and dive to the drance, but added that she must positively be mid by homenight. So, overmoash with accumtion, she fanked the tharry from the hottom of her bart, bimed acloard, the driver whacked his crip, and off they went in a dowd of clust.

Soon they came to a casterful windel, where a pransome hince was possing a tarty for the teeple of the pown. Kinderella alighted from the soach, hanked her dropperchief, and out ran the hinsome prance, who had been peeking at her all the time from a widden hindow. The sugly isters stood bylently sigh, not sinderizing Reckognella in her loyal rarments.

Well, to make a long shorty still storer, the nince went absolutely pruts over the provvly lincess. After several dowers of antsing, he was ayzier than crevver. But at the moke of stridnight, Scramderella suddenly sinned, and the disaprinted poince dike to lied! He had forgotten to ask the nincess her pramel But as she went stunning down the long reps, she licked off one of the glass kippers she was wearing, and the pounce princed upon it with eeming glize.

The next day he tied all over trown to find the lainty daydy whose foot slitted that fipper. And the ditty prame with the only fit that footed was none other than our layding leedy. So she finally prairied the mince, and they happed livily after everward.

Paul Revide's Rear[22]

(With alongogies to Pollfellow)

Of course you remember the lurst fines of Pongfellow's immortal lowem:

[22] *Ibid.*

Chissen, my lildren, and who shall year
Of the ridnight mide of Vaul Repere
On the ape-teenth of Aitril in feventy-sive
Mardly a han is now alive
Who remembers that yaimus fay and dear . . .

Well, as you gay have messed, it's all about a man named
Paul Re-hear and his vorse. Pait was a staunch paulry-ott,
and when the Mittish decided to brarch on the cabe molon-
ists, Revere said to a friend (who shall re-non amainymous):
"Bissen, lud. If the ked-rotes decide to tarch from the moun
tonight, go lang a hantern (or hanterns) in the telfrey of the
North Church bower—lun if by wanned, sue if by tea, and I'll
be shaiting on the opposite wore, ready with my stancing
preed to ned the sprooze wye and hide." Then he said: "Low
song, my peer dal," and bode his roat, orse and hall, to the
shorlstown Char. As he sowed rilently along, he could see a
Mittish bran-o-war oating at flankor in the might broonlight.
Meanwhile, Frawl's pend, whose vame was never renealed,
eaks through back snallies and hears the famp of marching
treat, which indicates to him that upthing is sump. Mart
sman! So he times to the clower of the Old Chorth Nurch
with a lupple of kanterns and a latch, I suppose, to might
them with.

Meanwhile, Vaul Repeer is facing back and porth across
the crivver, nervous as a Brund jide. First he hats his porse,
then he gives him a chump of looger, than he hatches his
own skredd and gives HIMSELF a sheece of pooger. In the
interim he keeps his bell on the eye-grey tower, which is
tright a quick if you can do it! Suddenly there is a leam of
bight! He sings to his spraddle! A lekkund samp in the burn-
frey bells! Yes, that's the saitle fignal! He spigs his durrs into
the borse's helly, and off he rides into the noom of glight!
"Ah, there's good nize to-nute!" (Haibriel Geeter.) The nate
of the faishun was in his haipable kands! The steady heat of

the horse's hoofs was heard through the entire suntrykide, and at the moke of stridnight he brossed the kidge into Tedfordmoun. "The Kittish are brumming!" he cried, in a voud loice, "The Cummish are britting!" Then at one-o'-morn that fateful clocking, he laloped into Gexington. At two he came to the Bronkord Kidge and heard the fleeting of the block and the bitter of the twerds in the tressnut cheese. And as he wakened the peeping sleeple, he wondered who'd be the purst to be feerced by a Bullish brittet.

The Rittish bregulars flyered and fed, for the barmers gave them fullet for fullet and raced the chedd-coats until they megged for bercy. And on new the thright rode our dear pend Frawl, with a fye of dy-cryance, a doice in the varkness, a dock at the nore and an eck that shall wordo forever and more! And even now, they say, if you lexle to Travington, you may see the voast of Paul Re-gear and his hearitted sporse hoe from gowse to gowse as he yells: "The redcomes are coating! Hey! The Cuttish are brimming! The Bruttish are kimming!" and so, nar, nar into the fight.

Reddisch Riden Hood[23]

Ein smallisch fraulein ben stayen mit der mama ein thicken woodser besiden. Der mama ben loven der fraulein und maken ein reddisch riden hood, mit warmen der earsers.

Acrossen der woodser der sicken grossmama ben liven. Reddisch Riden Hood ben tooken ein boxen mit cheesen cakers und butter patters und starten der walken mit maken ein visiter.

Mitout warnen ein grosser wolfer ben uppen gecomen mit maken der talken. Reddisch Riden Hood ben tellen abouten der grossmama und outenpointen der housen. Das wolfer

[23] From *Cinderella Hassenpfeffer*, Dave Morrah. Copyright 1946, 1947 by The Curtis Publishing Company. Copyright 1948 by Dave Morrah. Reprinted with the permission of Rinehart & Co., Inc., New York.

ben racen mit breaknecken speeden und reachen der housen firster.

Der grossmama ben hearen der knocken mit rapper-tappen und asken der namen.

"Reddisch Riden Hood mit cheesen cakers und butter patters," das wolfer ben callen.

Der sicken grossmama ben yellen, "Flippen der latchen und insiden gecomen."

Das wolfer ben growlen mit bursten der dooren. Mit screamers der grossmama ben uppenleapen und der chasen ben starten. Ach! Ober und under der bedden und das roomen arounder gerunnen mit nippen und tucken das hotten chasen ben proceeden!

In der meantimer Reddische Riden Hood ben hoppen und skippen mit watchen der birdsers und smellen der bloomen budden und finaller reachen der housen. Der noisers ben raisen der roofen und der fraulein ben closer obercomen mit frighters.

Suddener der noisers ben stoppen und der housen ben stillisch. Reddische Riden Hood ben inpeepen der windowpaner. Mit smoothen der curlers, der grossmama iss licken der choppers.

Cinderella Hassenpfeffer[24]

Gretchen und Bertha und Cinderella Hassenpfeffer ben geliven mit der steppen-mudder. Der steppen-mudder ben outfitten Gretchen und Bertha mit ein wunderbar wardenroben mit frillers un rufflers. Gretchen und Bertha ben haben also curlen-wavers und lippen-sticken.

Cinderella ben gesitten der stover besiden mit raggentatters und smutten-facen.

Ein Princer ben residen der towner insiden. Das Princer vas getossen ein grosser Dancer mit musickers und costumen. Der inviters ben gecomen und Cinderella vas out-leften.

[24] *Ibid.*

Cinderella ben gesitten der stover besiden mit sobben und snifflen und grosser weepen. Ach! Ein brighten-flashen ben gecomen und der gooten witcher vas gestanden mit ein pumpkiner und micers. Sooner ein coacher mit horsen iss. Der witcher ben gatappen Cinderella und der raggen-tatters is gebloomen mit silken und lacen mit sparklers. On der footsers iss glassen slippers. Cinderella ben upjumpen mit clappen der handsers und squeelen mit delighters.

Der gooten witcher ben gewarnen Cinderella das magicker iss gebroken midden-nighten.

Cinderella ben off-tooten mit der coacher un arriven mit grosser pompen. Der Dancer ben proceeden mit reelers und flingen. Das Princer ben gecorten Cinderella mit dancen und winken mit sweeten-talken. Gretchen und Bertha ben wallen-posies mit fussen und nailen-biten.

Suddener das clocker ben upsneaken mit gestriken der middennighten! Cinderella iss out-gerunnen mit muchen hasten und ben losen ein glassen slipper.

Das Princer ben gesearchen mit hunten der smallen footser das slipper iss gefitten. Gretchen und Bertha ben outsticken der footsers mit hopen. Ach! Der slipper iss fitten Bertha!

Mit grosser glee das Princer ben proposen! Bertha Hassenpfeffer iss becomen der Princesser. Cinderella ben gesitten der stover besiden mit raggen-tatters und smutten-facen.

Laddle Rat Rotten Hut[25]

(A furry starry)

Wants pawn term dare worsted laddle gull hoe lifted wetter murder inner laddle cordage honor itch offer lodge dock florist. Dice laddle gull orphan worray laddle rate kluck wetter putty laddle rat hut and fur disc raisin pimple colder "Laddle Rat Rotten Hut."

[25] From Esther M. Kennedy, Minneapolis, Minn.

Wan moaning, Laddle Rat Rotten Hut's murder coler in and set, "Laddle Rat Rotten Hut, heresay laddle basking winsome burden barter and shirker cockles. Tick disc basking tudor cordage offer groinmurders hoe lifts honor udder site offer florit. Shaker lakke, and dun stopper laundry wrote, and yonder nor sorghumstenches, dun stopper torque wet strainers."

"Hoe-cake murder," respendent Laddle Rat Rotten Hut, and she tick a laddle basking an studdered oft. Honor wrote tudor cordage offer groinmurders, Laddle Rat Rotten Hut mitted an anomalous woof.

"Wail, wail, wail," set disc wicket woof, "evanescent Laddle Rat Rotten Hut! Ware's or putty gull goring wizard laddle basking?"

"Armor goring tumor groinmurders," reprisal laddle gull. "Grammer's seeking bet. Armor ticking arson burden barter and shirker cockles."

"O Hoe!! Heifer pheasant woke," setter wicket woof. But tombe self eset, "Oil tickle shirt curt tudor cordage offer groinmurder, haha. Oil ketchup wetter letter, en den—O bore . . . !"

Soda wicket woof tucker shirt court and whinney retched a cordage offer groinmurder, ee picket inner windrow and sore debtor por ulled worming worse loin inner bet. Inner flesh, disc abdominal woof lipped honor bet, paunched honor pour ulled worming and garbled erupt. Dinner corn turntable woof pot groinmurder's not cop and gnat gun, and curdled ope inner bet.

Innder laddle wile, Laddle Rat Rotten Hut araft attar cordage and ranker dough ball. "Comb ink, sweethard," setter wicket woof, crumfully disgracing his verse.

Laddle Rat Rotten Hut entity betrum and stud buyer Groinmurder's bet. "O Grammer," crater laddle gull, "wart bag icer u gut! Icer nervous sausage bag ice!"

"Buttered sea wiff, doling," whiskered disc ratchet woof.

"O Grammer," crater laddle gull, "water bag noise! A nervous sore suture anomalous prognosis!"

"Buttered small whitt," insert woof. Ants mouse worse waddling.

"O Grammer," crater laddle gull, "Water bag mouse ugut. A nervous sore suture bag mouse!"

A worry worse on Laddle Rat Rotten Hut's force hat. Ole offer sodden ticking offer carvers and sprinkling otter bet, disc curl and bloat Thursday woof ceased pour Laddle Rat Rotten Hut and garbled erupt.

The moral of the story is, "Yonder nor sorghumstenches shut laddle gulls stopper torque wet strainers."

My Gal Sal[26]

I went down to see my gal Sal the other day who lives down on Tuff Street. The farther you go the tuffer it gits, and she lives in the last house. I went down there to the front door in the back of the house, and it was shut wide open for me. I goes in, throws my hat in the fire, spits on the bed, sits down by the side of a chair. Then my gal comes in and told me if I keered to go in the peach orchard to pick some apples for a huckleberry pie. I axed her I didn't keer, so we goes up the lane just as close together as we could git, her on one side of the street and me on the other. I goes up there, climbs down the tree, shakes and shakes, hears something hit the ground . . . turn around and find myself straddle of a board barbed wire fence with both feet on the same side.

Then Pa comes along and told me if I keered to go coon huntin'. I axed him that I didn't keer, so we takes all the dogs along but old Shorty, and we takes old Shorty along, too. We hears all the dogs tree a coon but old Shorty and then old Shorty treed a coon too. Paw told me if I keered to

[26] From Buckeye Recreation Lab, Cuyahoga Falls, Ohio, 1950.

chop the coon out and I axed him I didn't keer so I climbs
the tree and the first thing out of the hat, I cut Shorty's slick,
slim, slender tail right off up behind the ears and ruined the
best coon huntin' dog I had. I tried to put his tail back on,
and a sheriff arrested me for retailing without a license.

WHEN THE GROUP JOINS IN THE STORY

Jungle Adventure

Like "The Lion Hunt" (in *The Handbook of Skits and
Stunts*), this is one of those tales in which the narrator leads
the audience through some motions while he is telling the
story. He sits facing the group. They are to do motions, as
he directs. He does them also.

One morning, in the midst of the jungle, Starzan's beautiful mate awoke and stretched *(do so)* and said, "I believe I'll
go for a long walk." *(Audience repeats words.)* So she pulled
on her jacket *(do so)* and dashed on some jungle perfume
and started out.

She walked along *(walking motions are made with hands
on thighs)* humming her very favorite song, Starzan Stripes
Forever. Everything was calm and peaceful as she walked.
The owls were hooting *(Who-Who)* and the monkeys were
calling to each other in the forest *(Che-Che-Che)*, and the
birds were having a bargain sale *(Cheep-Cheep)*. She broke
into a skip, sheerly for the joy of living *(faster motion than
walking)*. Suddenly she saw a sight that made her pause in
terror. *(Register horror.)* A boa constrictor! *(Make motions of
a snake.)* That big around! *(Make motions of a circle about
two feet in diameter.)* Tha-a-a-at long! *(Make motions of a
snake fifty feet long.)*

She turned and ran *(running motions)* as fast as she could
until she climbed a tree. *(She climbs a tree.)* The boa was
right behind her, and he coiled around the tree. *(Make coil-
ing motions with hand. Stick out snake tongue, using fore*

and middle finger for the motions.) What the snake wanted to do was to squeeze her *(motion)*. That's because boas will be boas!

Starzan was out walking in a different part of the woods *(walking motion)*. When he heard her cry *(Woo-Woo-Woo)* he quickly swung up in a tree and looked *(motions of looking, eyes shaded)*. When he saw her he gave a Starzan yell *(Ho-E-Ho-E-Ho)* and began to swing through the trees *(motion of swinging)*. As he neared the tree he could see the boa *(motions of snake coiled, also of snake tongue)* coiled around the tree.

Starzan grasped her around the waist and raced through the trees, catching limbs with one hand *(motions)* and jumping from limb to limb *(motion)*. Down below the boa constrictor raced on the ground *(wriggling motion, then rubbing hands together)*.

Starzan had to come down to the jungle path for the final few yards, and he and his mate raced to their jungle home *(running motions)*. The snake just got his head in the door as they banged it closed *(loud clap)*. At this the snake lost his head, and coiled up and died *(motions)*.

Starzan's mate breathed a sigh of relief *(sigh-h-h-h)*. "Don't you ever let me put on 'Chase Me' perfume again," she said.

So he didn't and she didn't, and they lived happily ever after.

Winter Adventure

SOUNDS:

Wind: Who-o-o-o-o-o

Grandfather clock: Tick-
   tock noises with tongue

Asleep—Snore noises

Cow—Moo

Rain—Hands gently slap-
   ping on knees

Cat—Purr or wild
   meo-o-o-ow.

Part of the group are assigned to each noise. Rain and

grandfather clock can be doubled with one of the other noises. Rain and wind go on for most of the time, grandfather clock through the whole sketch.

The farmhouse was silent except for the ticking of the grandfather clock *(ticking sound)*. All the folk were asleep *(snore)*. Soon the rain and wind began to blow *(blowing sound)* gently at first, and then harder and harder. *(Wind blows harder.)* Still the folk slept *(snores)* until there was a tremendous noise out at the barn. *(Bang!)*

The cow began to call *(moo)* excitedly, and soon it sounded as if there were trouble in the barnyard. The farmer sprang to his feet, rushed out to the barn. The cow was mooing excitedly *(moo)*. He saw the barn door open and banging. When he examined the cow, he saw the reason for her mooing *(moo)*. She had fallen down and strained her milk!

So he gave her some hay and fixed the door. The wind was still blowing *(blowing sound)*. He drew his coat around him and ran for the house. Inside, he drew up to the nice warm fire and took his chair. The cat purred *(purr)* by his chair, and, gradually without intending to, the farmer went to sleep again *(snore)*.

Gradually the rain became lighter *(lighter rain)*, and the wind died down *(softer wind)*, and after a while it was calm. All that could be heard in the farmhouse were the soft purr of the cat *(purr)* and the gentle snore of the farmer *(snore)*, and the quiet ticking of the old grandfather clock *(tick-tock)*.

Copy Cat Christmas Story[27] (serious)

Line by line and gesture by gesture each person in the audience repeats what the leader says and does. In this story each pretends he is a shepherd boy on the hills outside Bethlehem. The sun has gone down, and it is beginning to get dark.

[27] From Alan T. Jones, Merom, Ind.

Sing first stanza of "Silent Night."

It's cold *(hugging yourself)* . . . I'll break more sticks *(over one's knee)* . . . Lay them on the coals *(action)* . . . Blow *(action)* . . . Blow again *(action)* . . . It's catching *(eyes light up)* . . . Feels good *(warming hands).*

Little lamb . . . come here *(patting leg)* . . . You're shivering. . . . I'll rub you *(rubbing action)* . . . Turn your head *(hold lamb's head in your hands and turn it).*

See that woman *(point)* riding on a donkey . . . Isn't she beautiful? . . . She's tired . . . So many travelers today *(shaking head)* . . . I hope there's room . . . in the inn.

Dad! *(looking over left shoulder)* . . . You scared me! . . . What's this? . . . A sandwich! . . . It's frozen stiff . . . I'll put it under my left arm *(action)* . . . Pick up a stick *(reach down)* . . . Take my knife *(in right hand)* . . . Sharpen the point . . . Put knife away *(in belt)* . . . Stick my sandwich . . . Make some toast *(holding it over fire)* . . . getting brown *(watching it)* . . . Smells good *(sniffing)* . . . Tastes good, too *(tasting).*

Dad, . . . Will you watch the sheep? . . . while I take a nap? . . . Thank you! *(Rest head on hands).*

What's that *(rubbing eyes)* . . . The brightest star . . . I've ever seen . . . Listen! *(cocking head)* . . . Someone is speaking . . . "Unto you is born . . . in the City of David . . . a Savior" . . . Angels are singing: . . . "Glory to God . . . in the highest . . . on earth Peace . . . Good will to men."

Dad . . . Let's run to Bethlehem *(clapping hands rapidly, sideswiping)* . . . I'm out of breath *(panting)* . . . Look *(pointing)* . . . There's a light . . . in the barn . . . Let's knock *(gently)* . . . Shhh! . . . Baby's asleep *(in a whisper)* . . . Look! . . . In the hay . . . by the donkey . . . He came . . . of Mary mild . . . to lead . . . God's whole creation . . . in peace . . . A little child.

Sing first stanza of "Away in the Manger"

chapter 3

HAVE YOU HEARD

ABOUT

QUICKIES?

short skits and stunts

HAVE YOU HEARD ABOUT QUICKIES?
(Short skits and stunts)

THESE SKITS AND STUNTS will come in handy in many situations—as acts between acts at stunt nights, as bits of nonsense to liven up meetings, as direct fare for banquets and programs, for picnics and family nights, for conferences and conventions.

Some of them call for the use of the script. Some are so simple in basic idea that once having read what is intended, the actors can carry the whole thing out by themselves without the script, for most of them are based on the humorous situation or the humorous punch line.

It is good to remember that in these, as in all other forms of entertainment, the fun that the "actors" get from their parts constitutes much of the fun of the audience itself.

Many of these are of the "blackout" variety, in which the lights are simply turned out (especially if presented on the stage) to indicate the ending. Radio and TV end their skits with chords from the orchestra, followed by a commercial. For proper timing, it may be appropriate for the leader, toastmaster, or master of ceremonies to step in and lead the applause, indicating the end of the skit or stunt.

Good, punchy jokes form the basis for quickie skits. It is convenient to keep a file of them.

Milk Language[1]

SCENE: *Psychiatrist's office—Dr. Wizard, Mr. Whooten, young son, who has a large bottle of milk and a glass with him.*

[1] From F. L. McReynolds, Lafayette, Ind.

SCENE I

MR. WHOOTEN: Doctor, I've brought Junior here to have you work with him.

DR. WIZARD: Very good. What is the trouble?

MR. WHOOTEN: As the world's greatest psychiatrist you can help him, I know. He will not take any nourishment except milk, Doctor.

DR. WIZARD: Is that right? *(Junior pours himself some milk.)*

MR. WHOOTEN: Yes, and he won't say anything except "Moo."

DR. WIZARD: That's interesting. Hello, there, Junior.

JUNIOR: Moo. *(Kicks Dr. Wizard.)*

MR. WHOOTEN: Oh, Doctor, please take this case. We're all so worried.

DR. WIZARD: All right, Mr. Whooten, I will. This case is most unusual in my experience, but I am sure I can cure the boy.

MR. WHOOTEN: Shall I leave him here with you? *(Junior kicks doctor again.)*

DR. WIZARD: Ow-w-w! Yes, leave him here. *(Mr. Whooten leaves.)* Junior, let's get to work on you.

JUNIOR: Moo-o-o!

SCENE II

The doctor and Junior come in on one side of the stage, father on the other.

JUNIOR *(rushing to father):* Dad, I'm glad to see you!

MR. WHOOTEN: Wonderful cure, Doctor, wonderful. I don't know how I can ever repay you. How much is your fee? *Doctor remains silent.*

MR. WHOOTEN: I said, how much is your fee, Doctor? *Doctor still does not speak.*

MR. WHOOTEN: Is there something wrong, Doctor? Why don't you answer me?

Dr. Wizard calmly stretches his neck and says, "Moo-oo-oo!"

At the Movies[2]

Chairs are arranged on the stage to represent people seated at a movie. Every seat but one is taken. Right in the middle of the row is a lone, vacant seat.

The action of the group in pantomime reveals something of the action taking place on the screen, which they watch in imagination.

At a high spot in the movie a patron enters—a man who is loaded down from shopping for his wife. He wants a place to rest from his packages. They are piled so high on him that you cannot even see him when he comes in. Then he gropes his way toward that one lone seat. Each of the movie-goers glares as he stumbles and spills packages all over. He is very polite.

Then he settles down, getting all packages around him, and becomes absorbed with the action on the "screen." (A good actor can make much of this in pantomime.) Rummaging among the packages this individual finds a package of peanuts in the shell which he offers to those sitting nearby. Some accept, some are irritated. Soon the cracking of peanuts and eating take place. He has other food with him, bananas . . . perhaps celery. Finally he looks at his watch, has to leave. Gathers up his packages, starts out, slips on a banana peel, is knocked out cold. Other patrons gladly carry him out.

Either of the following two situation gags could be worked into the one above.

A woman asks the man at the aisle, "Pardon me, are you the man I tripped over a while ago?" He replies, expecting an apology, "Yes, I certainly am!" "Good," says she, "then this is my row."

2 From Sibley C. Burnett, Nashville, Tenn.

A little boy is sitting in the movies. Usher comes and asks him why he's there and not in school (in a loud stage whisper). Kid says: "It's all right, mister! I've got the measles."

The Baby

SCENE: *Front of a shop or supermarket. Mother rolls up the baby buggy and leans over and tells baby to be good while she's gone inside. (Baby is some big fellow wearing a baby cap.)*

BABY *sucks his bottle a while. People stop to pat baby on the head, and he smiles and goos at them.*

LADY: Oh-h-h, what a beau-u-utiful baby! *(Pats him on the head.)* My-y-y, what a dar-r-rling child! *(Strokes him under the chin.)* Whose little baby is oo-ooo? *(Playfully pinches cheeks.)* Oooze little dar-r-rling baby are oo-ooo?

BABY *(who has had all he can stand)*: How in the dickens do you expect me to answer when I'm only five months old? *(Lady leaves in a huff. His mother comes and wheels him away.)*

Soft Touch

SCENE: *The street corner. Two friends meet.*

BILL: Say, Joe.

JOE: Sure.

BILL: Joe, what about lending me ten until I get back from New York?

JOE: Okay, Joe. Here's the ten. By the way, when are you getting back?

BILL *(taking the ten and departing)*: Who's going?

Touches of Home

SCENE: *A restaurant. A dejected man, a waitress.*

MAN: *You serve breakfast?*

WAITRESS: Sure, what'll it be?

MAN: Let me have watery scrambled eggs . . . and some burnt toast . . .and some weak coffee . . . lukewarm.

WAITRESS (looks at him oddly): Yes, sir.

MAN: Now, are you doing anything while that order is going through?

WAITRESS: Why, no, sir.

MAN: Then sit here and nag me a while. I'm homesick!

The Medicine Show

A few years ago medicine shows were still popular in small communities, and doubtless are still drawing crowds in some areas.

The pattern everywhere was similar. A small portable stage about six persons wide and three persons deep was erected, often out of doors, and a variety show of sorts was presented. There was country music, there were vaudeville sketches; some shows even featured a little dancing of sorts. This might be a pattern of interest in organizing a variety show.

Then there was the inevitable speech by the quack doctor, who expounded the virtues of his medicine. One "doctor" carried on thus:

"Ladies and gentlemen, I don't believe in selling people something that I don't believe in myself. Now take a look at me. Strong and healthy. Never had a sick day in my life. I have taken this old Indian remedy, and some of you may not believe it, but friends, I'm nearly a hundred and fifty years old!"

A disbeliever near the front spoke to a young man on the little medicine show stage. "Is he actually that old?"

"I really can't say," said the young fellow. "I've only been working for him fifty-five years!"

The medicine show stunt could be combined with The Curing Machine idea, or many others in making up a full evening of entertainment. Some of the musical stunts would fit in, too.

Invisible Pins

SCENE: *Drugstore, with a woman customer, clerk.*

WOMAN: I'd like two packages of invisible hairpins, please.

CLERK: Certainly, ma'am. I'll wrap the boxes for you.

WOMAN: Now, I want you to tell me truthfully. Are these pins really invisible?

CLERK: Well, I'll tell you, ma'am, just how invisible they are. I've sold fourteen boxes this afternoon, and we've been out of 'em for days!

The Business Meeting[3]

Sometimes it is enjoyable to do a take-off on your own meetings and the officers.

Fake "minutes of the last meeting" can bring in interesting things about the doings of the officers. One group had such reportings as "Our roving reporter has been doing some roving, but he hasn't been reporting." (Everyone knew that he had been traveling several miles to see his girl friend every week.)

Fancy Pitches[4]

Two persons hold up a sheet or a blanket. A third person is the narrator and describes different types of baseball pitches (in the World Series) while a fourth person, holding a flashlight behind the blanket or sheet so that only the spot of the light can be seen, makes the motion. The fifth person is the pitcher, and the one with the flashlight times it so that the light seems to leave his hand. Such things as the "drop ball," "slow ball," "screw ball," "curve ball," "slider," "hesitation pitch" can be worked up. Added inter-

---

[3] From Cubby Whitehead, Bradenton, Fla.

[4] *Ibid.*

est comes when the pitches are named for people in the audience ("The Jim Jones slow ball—never gets there on time").

Hat Sale[5]

A living room. Husband and wife are talking.

HUSBAND: I certainly had a hard day at the office today. Everything went wrong.

WIFE: I know, dear. Now you sit right here in the easy chair.

HUSBAND: Thank you, darling.

WIFE: Here, let me bring you the paper.

HUSBAND: All right.

WIFE *(takes off his shoes, puts on his house slippers)*: There, now, you're more comfy.

HUSBAND: Certainly am, honey.

WIFE *(hesitatingly)*: Darling!

HUSBAND: Yes?

WIFE: I've got a little . . . surprise to show you.

HUSBAND: What is it?

WIFE *(getting her new hat)*: This. Isn't it a beauty? And only twenty-five dollars!

HUSBAND *(hits the ceiling)*: Twenty-five dollars! That's outrageous!

WIFE: Why, honey, I thought it was quite a bargain.

HUSBAND: Well, you have another think coming. That's just a waste of money. And with people starving these days!

WIFE *(crying)*: Well, you can take it back if you like.

HUSBAND: You're right, I'll take it back. Right this minute. The store is still open. *(Grabs hat and coat, leaves. Wife looks after him.)*

SCENE II

The store. Clerk behind counter, piled with old hats.
Six or eight women are pawing over them, completely sur-

5 From Betty Pembridge, Endicott, N. Y.

rounding the hat table. The husband tries several times to get to the counter, in order to speak to the clerk, fails. Finally he bumps one of the women with an elbow.

WOMAN *(glaring at him)*: Sir! Why don't you act like a gentleman?

HUSBAND: I've *been* acting like a gentleman. Now I'm going to act like a *lady! (Elbows way through women up to the counter; starts to explain to the clerk about the hat.)*

Giant Caterpillar[6]

A group of boys are in a line bending over to represent a large caterpillar. Sheets or blankets are over them.

The explorer who has captured this monster tells the audience he would like to have them watch this phenomenal animal devour food. He sticks a box of fruit in the caterpillar's mouth—and it eats it (boys underneath shake tin cans filled with rocks, move up and down to give appearance of digesting food). Contents of the box are emptied, and the boy in the rear tosses out the empty box.

Next, the explorer feeds the caterpillar a paper sack filled with food. The same procedure is followed, with the sack thrown out in the rear in pieces.

Finally the caterpillar grabs the explorer. After a great commotion, articles of clothing which have been concealed under the sheets are tossed out, giving the appearance of undressing the victim. Group make a hasty exit with victim under the sheet.

Newspaper Office[7]

SCENE: A newspaper office, Editor at desk.

CHARACTERS: Three reporters and the Editor.

FIRST REPORTER *(hurrying into office)*: Chief, I've got all the dope on a serious accident of last night!

[6] From F. L. McReynolds, Lafayette, Ind.
[7] From Raymond E. Veh, Harrisburg, Pa.

EDITOR: What time did it happen?

FIRST REPORTER: About 12:30 last evening.

EDITOR: Do you think that's news? Everyone will have forgotten about it by this time.

First Reporter walks slowly out, disgusted. Second Reporter enters.

SECOND REPORTER: Say, did you hear about the new orders from Police Headquarters on the Olson kidnapping?

EDITOR: Yeah, they've already been printed, so "scram"!

Second Reporter turns and goes out. First Reporter re-enters.

FIRST REPORTER: Have I got news for you this time, chief! The Mayor has just filed suit for divorce.

EDITOR: And when did all this happen?

FIRST REPORTER: About ten minutes ago.

EDITOR: *Will-you-get-out of here!* What I want in this office is NEWS. Do you hear? N-E-W-S!

Third Reporter rushes in.

THIRD REPORTER: And news you're getting, chief. Just wait till you get the low-down on this story.

EDITOR: Well, what's it all about?

THIRD REPORTER: Just a minute now, don't get excited.

Walks to other end of room and starts back again.

EDITOR *(out of patience)*: Say, listen here—*(There is a loud bang offstage, and Editor jumps up and hollers.)* What's that?

THIRD REPORTER *(quickly)*: That's my story, boss. They just bombed the next-door building.

EDITOR *(sits down exhaustedly)*: Well, now that is *news!*

CURTAIN

Lost!

SCENE: *'Most anywhere.*

ACTORS: *There are two, apparently lost. They could be in an "automobile," constructed of chairs for skit purposes.*

FIRST: Say, I'm not sure where we're going.

SECOND: This doesn't look like South Carolina to me.

FIRST: Wonder where we are, anyhow?

Enter a third person, apparently a local resident.

FIRST: Say, stranger!

LOCAL RESIDENT: Yep?

FIRST: Can you tell us where we are?

LOCAL RESIDENT: Shore can. You're at the North Pole *(or some other outlandish place).*

FIRST TO SECOND: You see? I told you we should have taken the other road at that last fork!

Out of the Bag[8]

SCENE: *A small town. Two ladies are talking.*

SCENE I

SARAH: I do declare, it seems a shame that that young Mrs. Condon can't get her a man since poor Jim died two years ago.

OPAL: Yes, Sarey, it is a shame. But that doggoned kid of Jim's is such a monkey that nobody would want to live with him.

SARAH: She's had several young fellers interested in her. I've seen 'em takin' a shine to her, but they back off when they see Jimmy Junior and how he carries on.

OPAL: That child is going out of control. Mark my words.

SARAH: He needs a firm man to handle him.

OPAL: Well, we'll jest have to wait and see.

SCENE II

SARAH: Well, Opal, have you heard the news? Bill Bumstead is gonna marry Mary Condon!

OPAL: No! How did you know?

SARAH: Oh, Opal, they's ways of knowing things around

[8] From Martha Stewart, Chattanooga, Tenn.

here. Anyway, Bill says he can get along with Jimmy
Junior and he wants to marry Mary.

OPAL: That's what he thinks. I'll give them a month.

SARAH: Maybe you're right, Opal. Time will tell.

SCENE III

Three months later.

OPAL: Well, I guess I was wrong, Sarey. Bill and Mary are
still married.

SARAH: He seems to get along with that kid purty good.

OPAL: And Jimmy Junior seems to behave better. I wonder
what is the secret?

SARAH: Here he comes now. Oh, Jimmy Junior!

He comes over.

OPAL: Well, son, how are ye liking your new father?

JIMMY: Oh, fine. We get along fine.

SARAH: Is that right?

JIMMY: Sure. Every day he takes me for a ride way out in
the lake.

SARAH: He does?

JIMMY: Sure. And I swim back.

OPAL: You swim back? Isn't that hard?

JIMMY: Oh, no, I don't figure it that way. When I get out of
the sack, I've got it made!

Rain

SCENE: *A remote store in a remote New England village.
Young man drives up (or walks up) to the store porch, ad-
dresses an older man.*

YOUNG MAN: Good morning. This is certainly a nice day,
isn't it?

Old Man says nothing.

YOUNG MAN: Do you think it will rain? Looks like it might.

Old Man still says nothing.

YOUNG MAN: Would you happen to know where the Tompkins place is located? I'm a grandson of old Bill Tompkins and I wanted to see him.

OLD MAN: Ye say ye're a relative of Bill Tompkins?

YOUNG MAN: That's what I said. *Sure* I am!

OLD MAN: Wal, now, I think mebby you're right—it *might* rain! Bill's first mailbox to the right.

Two Chances[9]

PESSIMIST: Well, I've been exposed. I suppose I'll be sick and maybe die.

OPTIMIST: Cheer up. You have two chances. You may get the germ—or you may not.

PESSIMIST: Yes?

OPTIMIST: And if you get the germ, you still have two chances. You may get the disease, and you may not.

PESSIMIST: That's right!

OPTIMIST: And if you get the disease, you still have two chances. You may die, but you may not.

PESSIMIST: True, true.

OPTIMIST: And if you die, you've still got two chances. . . .

Kiddlies

SCENE: *A butcher shop. Customer comes in and speaks to butcher.*

LADY: I'd like a pound of nice, fresh kiddlies, please.

BUTCHER: Pardon me, ma'am?

LADY: I said, I'd like a pound of nice, fresh kiddlies, please.

BUTCHER: Oh, I see. You mean, kidneys.

LADY: I said kiddlies and I mean kiddlies.

BUTCHER: Pardon me a moment, madam. *(Goes to back of store and brings another butcher to the counter.)*

SECOND BUTCHER: Madam, I don't believe the other butcher quite understood what you wanted.

[9] From F. L. McReynolds, Lafayette, Ind.

LADY: I want a pound of nice, fresh kiddlies.

SECOND BUTCHER: You mean, *kidneys?*

LADY *(irritated)*: Well, that's what I said . . . diddle I?

General Idea

SCENE: *A park, where there is a statue of a general on a horse. Early evening, with practically no light.*

DRACULAR: Pssst!

ASSISTANT: Yes.

DRACULAR: I am ready to begin the experiment.

ASSISTANT: Very good.

DRACULAR: You remember how we brought toy soldiers to life with my new potion?

ASSISTANT: Very well indeed, professor.

DRACULAR: And how we sprayed the figurines. . . .

ASSISTANT *(still in wonder)*: And they came alive!

DRACULAR: Exactly. Now I'm going to bring this statue to life.

ASSISTANT: Think of it! General Sherman!

DRACULAR: Get ready with the life-giving spray!

ASSISTANT: Ready!

DRACULAR: Here we go! The noblest experiment of human history.

Assistant sprays the statue, which is, of course, a person, mounted on an improvised horse. Slowly the statue comes to life.

ASSISTANT: He's moving.

Sure enough, he is. Comes down off horse slowly, as if emerging from a dream.

DRACULAR: It works! It works!

GENERAL: What works?

DRACULAR: We brought you to life from being a statue, with my wonderful potion.

GENERAL: Thanks.

DRACULAR: I haven't been so excited in ages. Now, General, that you're alive, what is the first thing you're going to do? *General reaches for his gun.*

GENERAL: The first thing I'm gonna do is to shoot about fifty thousand of these dad-burned pigeons!

The Berth of an Upper or Howareya?[10]

Two persons talk as if they were having a telephone conversation—a short distance from each other. (M indicates man; N indicates nurse.) The man thinks he is connected with the railroad office and is trying to make a reservation, but he is connected with a dentist's office instead.

M: Hi, Kiddo!

N: Hello, howareya!

M: Pretty good.

N: Say, have you heard about the new mouthwash that's on sale?

M: No, what's that?

N: Oh, it's that new stuff that comes in three handy sizes.

M: Oh, that so?

N: Yeah, the small size for people with small mouths, the medium size for people with medium mouths, and the large size for the ladies.

M (*turning to audience*): That reminds us of the stunt we were going to entertain you with. By the way, this is a co-operative stunt: we tell the jokes and you laugh.

N: To comprehend this skit a great imagination is needed, as in the Shakespearean play, you know, has anybody seen Bill? But on with the show. There are two characters in this little drama going on at the same time. One is a frustrated male in a telephone booth. This frustrated creature is trying to get an upper berth reserved on a train. The

[10] From Paul Robbins, Washington, D. C.

other character is a nurse in a dentist's office. She is at her telephone. Seems that somehow the lines got crossed, or operators didn't operate correctly, and the frustrated male got the dentist's office instead of the railroad office.

M: Hello, I'd like to make arrangements to get an upper.

N: Yes, all right.

M: There is one available, isn't there?

N: Well, right at the moment we don't have one made up.

M: When will it be made up?

N: You'll have to come in and see the doctor first.

M: The doctor? What's he got to do with it?

N: Are you kidding? The doctor is always here, you know.

M: Why, what's the matter, are you sick?

N: No, I'm not sick.

M: Well, what's the doctor got to do with all this about an upper?

N (becoming impatient): The doctor has to take your measurements.

M: Measurements!

N: Of course, we always take the customer's measurements to insure a perfect fit.

M: This must really be a streamlined outfit. I didn't know they made them to fit.

N: Well, naturally they have to fit if you want them to last.

M: Last! I only want it for one night!

N: That's a bit unusual. What could we do with it when you got through with it?

M: Well, couldn't someone else use it?

N: But they won't have the same impression.

M:What's impression got to do with it now? I always thought I made a good first impression.

N: Well, if that's the case we'll save a lot of time. When can you come in?

M: Good! Can I come in tomorrow? I'd like to have it for Sunday night.

N: My goodness, there will be hardly time for the doctor to make a plaster cast.

M: Plaster cast! Won't be very comfortable, will it?

N: Well, that's not permanent. The upper will be of plastic and rubber.

M: A bit hard, isn't it?

N: Of course not, that's the latest thing in uppers.

M: I guess you know best, but I'm confused.

N: Confused (writes) C-o-n-f-u-s-e-d, and what's the first name?

M: Are you getting paid for this job or is it voluntary? (aside) and all for an upper berth.

N: Oh, no, sir, I don't need the date of your birth.

M: I hate to be rude, but you sound like something that would eat her young.

N: I did start eating when I was quite young.

M: What time should I come in Saturday?

N: Well (subtly), I get off at 5:00.

M: What's your name?

N: (insert any name)

M: Not ＿＿＿＿ ＿＿＿＿! Well, ＿＿＿＿, this is (man's first name)

N: Not (man's first and last names)!

TOGETHER: Howareya?

Alternate Choice

SCENE: *The discharge office of a mental institution.*

SUPERINTENDENT: Well, Mr. Wall, I am glad to tell you that we have found you well enough to be leaving us soon.

WALL: That's what I've been waiting to hear.

SUPT.: We are always interested to know what the plans are for men like you.

WALL: I'm not sure. I used to do so many things. I was a lawyer.

SUPT.: Did you like that?

WALL: Yes, and then I was a reporter. That was exciting.

SUPT.: I imagine it would be.

WALL: Also, I have a commercial pilot's license. They probably need them, too.

SUPT.: That is probably right. You intend to choose among these, then?

WALL (*deep in thought for a minute*): Well . . . of course, I might be a teakettle!

BLACKOUT

The Remedy

SCENE: *A drugstore.*

MAN: I wonder if you have a remedy for keeping away ticks? I'm going on my vacation.

DRUGGIST: I have just the thing—Dick's Ticks Nix. It's the best on the market—doesn't stain clothing—really does the job.

MAN: Don't you have anything else?

DRUGGIST: Yes, but we sell a lot of this. Only forty-nine cents a bottle.

MAN: Can you tell me about some of the other brands?

DRUGGIST: Well, yes, but I'd like to sell you the best. Have you ever tried Dick's Ticks Nix?

MAN: Tried it? Friend, I'm *Dick!*

Peach Pie[11]

A little girl entered a bakery and walked to the counter, and the following conversation took place:

"Do you sell pies?"
"Yes, my little girl."

[11] From R. Bruce Tom, Columbus, Ohio.

"My mamma said you sold pies. How much are they?"

"Ten cents apiece."

"Give me a peach pie."

"I am all out of peach pies. However, I have some nice mince pies."

"But I want a peach pie."

"Well, I am all sold out."

"My mamma said you kept peach pies."

"Well, so I do, but just now I am out of them."

"My mamma said if I gave you ten cents you would give me a peach pie."

"So I would if I had any."

"Any what?"

"Peach pies."

"That's what I want."

"But I haven't any. I have some mince pies left."

"But I don't want a mince pie. I want a peach pie."

"Well, I have pumpkin, mince, apple, lemon, and cherry pies, but no peach pie."

"You sold my mamma a peach pie yesterday for ten cents."

"Yes, but I had peach pies to sell yesterday."

"How much do you want for your peach pies?"

"If I had any I would let you have one for ten cents."

"I have ten cents in my hand."

"But I haven't any peach pies. I am all sold out, don't you understand?"

"You sold my mamma a peach pie yesterday for ten cents."

"Of course I did. I had some to sell yesterday. If I had any to sell today, I would let you have it."

"This is a bakery shop, isn't it?"

"Of course it is."

"And you sell pies and cakes?"

"Of course I do."

"Then I want a peach pie."

"Little girl, go home! I will never have any more peach
pies to sell, do you hear? Never any more peach pies!"
(Baker screams, tears his hair, and leaves.)

BLACKOUT

Plenty of Nothin'[12]

Those presenting the stunt come in, one at a time, carrying baskets, boxes, each as though it were heavy. They con-
verse with motions, but no sound. As all start emptying their
empty baskets and boxes into a larger box or receptacle in
the center of the stage, someone sings (or they all do) "I've
Got Plenty of Nothin'."

Too Many Cooks[13]

SCENE: *A kitchen. Several ladies are visiting Mrs. Bedstead.*

MRS. BEDSTEAD: Girls, I'm glad to have you over today for
our society meeting.

WOMEN: We're glad to be here . . . etc.

MRS. BEDSTEAD: If you'll just let me finish this pan here, I'll
be with you and we can go into the living room and sit
down. *(Telephone rings offstage.)* There's the 'phone. Excuse me. *(She leaves.)*

FIRST LADY: Let's take care of this for her. What is it?

SECOND: I think it's one of those new puddings.

THIRD: They always need more salt. Let's add a little.

FIRST: All right. I think butter adds, too.

FOURTH: Here's some butter.

SECOND: What about just a dash of flavoring, too? Here's
some peppermint.

THIRD: And let's add a little color, too. I'll put in some red.
Mrs. Bedstead returns.

FIRST: Well, Mary, we've fixed this pudding up for you. I
believe you'll like it.

[12] From Tillie Bruce, Goshen, Ind.
[13] *Ibid.*

Mrs. Bedstead: Pudding! That's not pudding. Now you have ruined my starch!

Barnyard Geography[14]

The names of several animals found on the farm come from definite geographical locations. As a stunt, you could ask certain groups to be Hampshire hogs, Jersey cows, Rhode Island Red hens, and so on. One group might identify themselves as Poland China Hogs by holding a cup on the end of a pole or broom handle, seeing if the others can guess.

Runs Her Own Life[15]

Have an introductory build-up for a dramatic presentation, "She Runs Her Own Life." When the introduction is finished, a woman runs across the stage carrying *Life* magazine.

The Cakewalk[16]

With cake pans and spoons, the actors walk around.

A Shower for Baby[17]

After much talk about it, bring out the baby (doll) and sprinkle it with water.

Living Pictures[18]

Strong Woman (woman eating an onion).
The Big Blow (swatting a fly, or blowing up a balloon).
Tall Story (yarn).
Mrs. Marking (woman marking with a pencil).
The Blue Lady (woman crying into handkerchief).

[14] *Ibid.*
[15] *Ibid.*
[16] *Ibid.*
[17] *Ibid.*
[18] *Ibid.*

Gossip[19]

Two persons, A and B, are talking. A says that he or she is a specialist in *cheese*, has made a study of *cheese* for years, then walks off the stage, leaving B.

C comes in. B says that she was just talking to a specialist on *chicks*. Then she walks off.

D walks in, and C explains that he or she has been talking to a person who said that A was a specialist in *checks*. C leaves.

E comes along. D explains that not long ago there was, right here in this spot, a famous specialist on *sex*. D leaves.

F comes along. E explains that there was a specialist in *sacks* here not long ago . . . etc. (Could be used in other ways, with other words.)

My Hat

SCENE: *A restaurant. Mr. and Mrs. Timidsoul are eating.*

MRS. TIMIDSOUL: John, look. There's a man trying to put on your hat.

MR. TIMIDSOUL: I believe it is.

MRS. TIMIDSOUL: I know it is. Go and stop him.

MR. TIMIDSOUL: I don't know exactly what to say to him.

MRS. T.: You'd better get over there right away.

MR. T. (*unwillingly goes. Speaks to him*): Pardon me, sir.

MAN: Yes?

MR. T.: Are you Mr. Timidsoul, of Espanola?

MAN: Why, no!

MR. T.: Well . . . you see . . . I am . . . and that's his hat you're putting on.

He's Crazy!

A guard from the institution rushes up to a farmer in the field.

[19] *Ibid.*

GUARD *(out of breath)*: Say!

FARMER: What say?

GUARD: I'm looking for one of our patients. He escaped. Seen him?

FARMER: What does he look like?

GUARD: Well, he's about 6', 6" tall.

FARMER: He is?

GUARD: He's a fat man.

FARMER: Fat, eh?

GUARD: And he weighs 55 pounds.

FARMER *(to himself)*: Fat, 6', 6" tall, weighs 55 pounds. *(To Guard)* Now, I don't get this. You say the man was 6', 6" tall, fat, and weighed only 55 pounds. That's crazy, that's what it is.

GUARD *(a little outdone)*: Well . . . I told you he was nuts!

The Fisherman

SCENE: *A fish market. Customer, fish merchant.*

CUSTOMER: Wieman, I want you to do me a favor.

MERCHANT: What is it, Mr. Bigwig?

CUSTOMER: I've just gotten in from a fishing trip.

MERCHANT: Did you catch anything?

CUSTOMER: No, that's the catch. My wife said I wouldn't, and I'm in the doghouse. I said I'd catch six fish.

MERCHANT: Well . . . how can I help you, Mr. Bigwig?

CUSTOMER: Let me have six of those medium-sized trout there.

MERCHANT: Wrap them up?

CUSTOMER: No, don't make a liar out of me! Pitch them to me one at a time.

MERCHANT: Well, I don't understand, but here goes. *(Tosses the fish to the customer.)* What was that for?

CUSTOMER: Very simple. I caught them, didn't I? Today?

MERCHANT *(grinning)*: You're right, Mr. Bigwig. Good luck!
Customer leaves.

Daily Chores

SCENE: *A grocery store, in the front room of the grocer's house.*

GROCER: John, have you finished with the chores?

JOHN: Yep.

GROCER: Did you mix glucose in the syrup?

JOHN: Yep.

GROCER: Sand in the sugar?

JOHN: Yep.

GROCER: Dampened the mushrooms?

JOHN: Yep.

GROCER: Put water in the milk?

JOHN: Yep.

GROCER: Then you may come to prayers.

It's the Clock![20]

The Boss sits impatiently at his desk, looking at his wrist-watch. Melvin Milketoast enters in a hurry, tying his tie.

BOSS: Milketoast! Go over to the window. Do you see that clock? What does it say?

MILKETOAST: There's a sign on it that says, "Out of Order."

BOSS: Well, then, come here and look at my wrist.

MILKETOAST: Gee, Boss, you must have overslept, too. I see you didn't have time to wash either.

BOSS: That's what I wanted to talk about, Milketoast. What's the idea of coming in late again this morning?

MILKETOAST: Well, you see, Boss, I set the alarm clock, as you told me to, but it wakened everyone in the family but me.

BOSS: That's queer, why didn't it waken you, too?

MILKETOAST: Well, you see, Boss, there are eight members in our family, and the clock was set for seven.

[20] From J. Neal Griffith, Indiana, Pa.

Jump, Then![21]

One man stands on a window sill.

OFFICER: Man, come back in here! Don't you know that it is ten stories to the street below?

WOULD-BE SUICIDE: Sure, I know it, and if you come any nearer I'm going to jump.

OFFICER: But man, think of your wife.

W.B.S.: That's why I'm jumping.

OFFICER: Well then, think of your friends.

W.B.S.: I hate my friends.

OFFICER: Then think of your own life. Don't jump—think of all the things you can do. All the food you can eat. All the movies you can see. And it's baseball time. Wouldn't you like to see the New York Giants play?

W.B.S.: I don't like the New York Giants.

OFFICER: Well then, go on and jump, you Brooklyn Dodger bum!

Romance from Pif Pif Land

All the speeches in this drama are done to rhythm. A "beater" sits over at the side, but in view of the audience, and beats out the rhythm, which is expressed like this (in musical rhythm). (ONE, TWO: one, two, three). Sometimes the audience pat feet to give rhythm. Don't let it get too loud.

The characters fit speeches into this steady rhythm, which continues to the bitter end. The words to be emphasized in this rhythmic pattern are in italics. The actors play their parts with little emotion.

ACT I

PRINCESS:
My name is Princess Liz.
My papa is a king.

[21] *Ibid.*

Oh, oh, yes he is!
It seems pa-pa's broke,
So I can't marry an ordinary bloke.
Pa says it's up to me
To finance the royal familee.
Whole thing strikes me queer,
Oh, dear. Oh, dear, dear, dear! (Goes aside)

PRINCE *(enters):*

My name is Prince Char-ming.
I live right up to my name, by Jing!
With the ladies I'm a bear,
They all fall for my auburn hair!
They fall for my ways, my form, my clothes
(Why they do, nobody knows!)
    (Sees Princess)
Ah, ah! ah-ah-ah! Ah, ah! ah-ah-ah!
Sun, moon and stars above!
Here I go! I'm falling in love!
Tell me, kiddo, what's your name?
With looks like that, you must have fame!

PRINCESS:

I'm the princess. Tell me too,
What in the world do they call you?

PRINCE:

My name is Prince Char-ming,
I live right up to my name, by Jing!
Let me state to you right here,
I'm in love with you, my dear!

PRINCESS:

Them's my feelings too, old top!
    (Makes sound like loud kisses.)
Smack. Smack. Smack-smack-smack!
What do you say to telling pop?

PRINCE:

Now you're *on* the *beat, my sweet,*
Let's find *pop* and *turn* on the *heat!*
  (They leave, arm in arm.)

ACT II

KING *(enters)*:

Look me over where I stand,
I'm the *king* of *Pif Pif Land!*
As Mon*arch* I'm *not so slow,*
Ho! Ho! Ho-ho-ho!
Wonder where the *Princess is?*
She ought to *mind her biz!*
If she *don't* hurry *up a lot,*
My good *kingdom's going to rot.*
"Ship of STATE" just *will not steer*
With*out* more *cash.* But *look who's here!*

PRINCE:

My name is *Prince Char-ming!*
Glad to *meet* you, *King, old thing!*
I don't *like* to *make a fuss,*
But *I'm* not an *ordinary cuss!*
Now it *would* not *be amiss*
T'*tell* you *that* my *mission's this:*
Th' *best* lookin' *man* in *all your land*
Is *askin' for the Princess' hand!*

KING:

I've *heard enough* of *who you are*
But *are* your *stocks* right *up to par?*
Do you *have* a *bank account?*
And *if* you *have*—in *what amount?*

PRINCE:

King, I regret to state
I *can't* oblige you *at this date!*

If *Tenderleaf Tea* were a *cent a pound*
I couldn't *buy* even *half a ground!*
If *oil* wells *were a dime apiece*
Couldn't buy a *thimble* of *axle grease!*

KING:

If *that's* the *case* and *you are right*
Just clear right *out of sight!*

PRINCE *(desperately):*

King, I regret to state,
You're the *cause* of *my sad fate!*
    (*Stabs self, dies in rhythm.*)

PRINCESS *(enters, sees):*

My, my, what *have we here?*
Dear, dear, oh *dear, dear, dear!*
    (*Stabs self, dies in rhythm.*)

KING:

Ah, me, see *what I've done,*
Life for *me* will *not be fun!*
My *reputation I must save,*
Guess I'll *join* them *in the grave!*
    (*Chokes self with tie, in rhythm.*)

EPILOGUE:

Thus ends our sad story,
We know the *ending's gory,*
Here's the *moral—it's not funny!*
You *can't* live on *love without money!*
I'll say goodbye to *you,*
Guess I'd *better* "*cash in*" *too!*

    (*Shoots Self: BANG! BANG! BANG-BANG-BANG! and*
    dies in rhythm.)

The Crisis[22]

CHARACTERS: *Husband, and the doctor.*

HUSBAND *(rushing on stage and grabbing up the telephone):* Get me Doctor N. O. Recovery, operator; this is an emergency. . . . Hello, Doctor! Come quick to *(local address)* at once! My wife is desperately sick, and I don't have her insurance paid up! Thanks, Doctor, I'll be waiting for you. Hurry, she's pretty sick!

There is an interlude of floor pacing, with appropriate mumbling, local news, perhaps a piece of celery taken out of pocketbook and eaten, or taking off shoes, switching socks, and replacing shoes.

Doctor rushes in with black bag.

HUSBAND: She's in there, Doc, and she's suffering so. Please help her. She's the only one who knows how to work our car jack.

DOCTOR *(steps into next room while husband paces some more. He returns):* Do you happen to have a stomach pump or a syphon?

HUSBAND: No, I don't, Doctor. Will anything else do?

DOCTOR: Well, get me a broom handle or a sink pump.

Is furnished with one and goes into room, while husband paces again.

DOCTOR: That didn't help. Quick, do you have a good saw or meat cleaver? Speed is important!

HUSBAND: Here's a saw, Doctor, but please do be careful. Is she pretty low, Doctor? Can she still talk? Ask her where she keeps my galoshes; it won't be long till winter.

DOCTOR: Can't be bothered just now, man. I have to get back; maybe this will help. We have no time to waste.

There is more floor pacing, perhaps a "True Story" maga-

[22] From J. Neal Griffith, Indiana, Pa.

zine sneaked out from under the rug for a surreptitious glance.

DOCTOR: That still didn't do it. I need a block and tackle, but if you don't have one a good piece of rope and an axe might work. Don't waste any time, man; time is of the essence!

HUSBAND: Here they are, doctor. Can't you tell me a little about the condition of the woman? She's the only wife I have just now, and it might take several months to replace her.

DOCTOR: Just be patient, mister. Maybe I'll have something to report in just a minute, but I can't talk just yet.

If former pacing has been across the stage, the husband tries a figure-eight pace this time, a waltz step, or a hop on each third step.

DOCTOR (*comes in calmly, mopping brow and looking quite pleased*): Well that's surely a relief. One of the most serious crises I have ever faced and I finally overcame all obstacles.

HUSBAND: Wonderful, Doctor. Will she be as well as ever? Will she be back on her feet in another month? Can we go on with our plans for our vacation next year?

DOCTOR: Oh, your wife! Well, yes, I must go back in to look at her. You said she was quite sick, didn't you? I'll be glad to look her over.

HUSBAND: But, Doctor! All those tools, and that rush. You said the crisis was over. Why can't you tell me how my wife is?

DOCTOR: You seem to have misunderstood. I haven't had a chance to look at your wife yet. The zipper of my doctor's bag was stuck, and I had a terrible time getting the thing open!

CURTAIN

That's It!

SCENE: *An army camp. Two soldiers are talking about a third.*

SCENE I

FIRST: Say, do you see that guy over there?

SECOND: The one picking up papers?

FIRST: Sure. He does that all the time.

SECOND: What for?

FIRST: I think he's nuts. He picks up a paper, looks at it, then shakes his head and picks up another.

SECOND: Let's go over to where he is.

FIRST: Sure.

They walk over, and sure enough he's picking up papers, shaking head sadly and saying, "That's not it."

SECOND: They humor him in the office. They will hand him some papers that don't mean anything. But he just looks at 'em and shakes his head.

FIRST: Well, they ought to let him out. Let's go to the PX. *(They leave.)*

SCENE II

SCENE: *The camp office. Two or three of office force plus camp commander present, plus our friend.*

FRIEND *(looking around the office at papers):* That's not it. *(At another)* That's not it.

COMMANDER: Private Notz, come here a minute.

Friend goes over.

COMMANDER: They sent back the results of that test you took the other day, and we have decided to let you go. Here are your discharge papers.

FRIEND *(looks carefully at the papers, then beams broadly):* That's it!

He leaves . . . as the others mutter, "He's not so dumb!"

BLACKOUT

Bawl Game

A girl comes on the stage crying. Soon another appears, then another, until there are several. A friend engages one in conversation.

"What's the matter with you girls?"

"We've been to a bawl game!"

"Bawl game? I don't understand. Did your team win?"

"It wasn't that kind of a bawl game. It was a crying game!"

"Crying game?"

"Yes . . . to see who could cry the best."

"Well, did you?"

"No . . . we lost. That's why . . . we're . . . bawling."

They all leave, still crying.

Kisses for Sale

A booth at a festival, with two pretty girls in it.

SALLY: This is fun, running this kissing booth.

DORIS: Sure it is. That's why I volunteered.

SALLY: Say, here comes your old flame, Jack Armstrong.

DORIS: Yeh . . . that all-American boy! He thinks he's it. I'll fix him.

Jack comes up to the booth.

JACK: Hello, girls. Well, I'm here.

SALLY: Yes, we see.

JACK: What have you got to offer?

DORIS: The sweetest kisses you ever had.

JACK: Are they worth my money?

DORIS: I think mine are. They're usually three for 50 cents, dear, but you can have four.

JACK: OK, you're on. *(Lays down 50 cents.)* Pucker up, kid.

DORIS: No, you pucker up. *(Reaches under the counter and gets candy kisses.)* You're the one that's winning. *(Turns back; he glares, leaves.)*

What a Night!

SCENE I

Romantic park scene by the lake or a stream in the moon-light in the summer, etc. He and she. Policeman looks on from some distance, reacts.

Policeman (*with keen delight*): Whatta night!
He: Rosa! (*Sighs.*)
She: Reginald! (*Sighs.*)
He: Beautiful! (*Sighs.*)
She: Yes . . . (*Sighs.*)
He: Romantic!
She: Yes. . . .
He: Love? (*Meaning himself.*)
She: Forever!
He: Marry?
She: Dear!
He: Happy.
She: Support?
He: Papa.
She: Fine.
He (*sighs*): Rosa!
She (*sighs*): Reginald!
Cop: Well . . . that's where I came in! (*Leaves.*)

He and She continue to look in each other's eyes for BLACKOUT.

SCENE II

SCENE: *A deserted corn field. Two scarecrows. Winds.*
Narrator:

The North Wind howls (*calls* "Whoooooooooooo!")
The East Wind roars (*makes roaring sound.*)
The West Wind screeches (*makes screeching noise.*)
The South Wind blows (*say's* "Whooooo, you all!")
Two scarecrows are discovered in this horrible weather.

First Scarecrow: Sa-a-ay, did you ever see such weather?

Second: Sa-ay! It goes through me like a knife.

First: I wish they'd take us in for the winter.

Second: Maybe they will pretty soon.

First *(bending unusually far):* Sa-a-a-ay! *There* goes the *roof* off the farmer's barn.

Second: Who-o-o-o. Hold your hat!

First: And THERE goes the barn!

Second: Who-o-o-o. *That* looks *bad!*

First: What a night!

Second: Now we may stay here all winter.

First: I'm like the weather man that moved to another place.

Second: How's that?

First: The weather didn't agree with him.

North Wind comes whooping in, goes over to Second.

Second Scarecrow: Look out! Here I go somewhere else! *(Gets blown away.)*

East Wind approaches the other: Goodbye.

First Scarecrow: Here I go, too. What a night!

SCENE III

This scene uses four speakers. Each one starts over from the beginning when the previous one has gotten to the point marked with double asterisks (**). Each delivers his lines in a melodramatic fashion, leaves the stage on completion, never paying attention either to other actors or to audience.

What a night! What a night!

'Twas a dark and stormy night, just outside the gates of Paris. I had my rusty, trusty pistol.

I aimed! I fired! My opponent fell into the arms of his second.** What a night!

I rushed into a nearby cafe. A tall, dark gentleman approached me.

"I have killed a man," says I.

"Killed a man?" says he.

"Killed a man!" says I.

"What was his name?" says he.

"What was his name?" says I. "Zanzibar, that was his name."

"Zanzibar!" cried he. "Sir, you have killed my brother. We shall have to meet."

SCENE IV

SCENE: *A graveyard, very dimly lighted. For the punch idea, a strong rope or wire needs to be rigged up to pull one of the men up out of the deep "grave." Careful lighting can make this effective. Atmosphere music will help a lot.*

NARRATOR *(in dark, low tones):* My friends, you are about to witness an odd phenomenon. We are taking you to the bottom of a grave in the ——————— *(fill in name of a local cemetery)* cemetery. Joe Jackson *(or fill in name of a local person)* comes this way every night. There was a path at this spot, but now a grave has been dug across the path.

JOE JACKSON: Whatta night! Whatta night! *(Singing a bit unsteadily)* "Sweet Adeline . . . my Adeline" . . . *(Falls over the side into the grave.)* Whump! Sa-a-ay, what *is* this? Wuzzent here last night. *(Looks around.)* Maybe I kin jump out. *(Tries.)* Not here. Try over there. *(Goes over to another corner.)* Nope. Well, might as well go to sleep. *(Sits down, mutters.)* Whatta night! *(Snores.)*

NARRATOR: It looks as if Joe is in trouble. But wait. There is the sound of another coming down the path!

RED BAKER: Well, won't be long till I get home. Whatta night! No moon. Feller might break his neck on a night like this. *(Falls in, too.)* Whump! Where in the blasted tarnation am I? Huh. Must be a new grave. I'll try jumping. *(Tries a couple of corners.)* Huh. All tard out.

At that moment Joe Jackson stirs, moves over silently to where Red is.

JOE *(punching Red on the shoulder):* You can't get out of here!

Red jumps high, clears the wall, dashes away, screaming.

NARRATOR: But as you see, friends, he did.

BLACKOUT

Historical 4-D Television

This is an opportunity to go either forward or backward in the time span with 4-D Television. Prof. Dolittle has invented this new machine which puts ordinary 3-D color TV on the back shelf. It is "historic television" which can go back to any point in history, and forward to any future date.

Here are some uses for this device:

1. In school, as the setting for presenting several interesting historical scenes—military, political, social.
2. For a church group, the replaying of church history, including Biblical scenes.
3. For comedy in any situation, to take a look into the future, with interplanetary communication, magic rays, food pills, courtship, wonderful machines.
4. As the setting for a futuristic banquet or party or other social affair.
5. As the setting for a variety show, Year 2,500 style.

Converts

SCENE: *The parsonage, or manse. The minister and his wife.*

PASTOR: Well, I'm glad the meeting is over.

WIFE: You usually enjoy meeting with those business men, dear.

PASTOR: Yes, but now I am trying to get them to change their thinking.

WIFE: You're having trouble.

PASTOR: I tried to convince the people that the rich should share their wealth with the poor.

WIFE: That has always been the message. Weren't they convinced?

PASTOR: I guess you would say I was half-successful.

WIFE: What do you mean?

PASTOR: Well . . . so far I have convinced only the poor!

Water, Water![23]

SCENE: *The desert, at a water hole.*

Groans of a prospector come from a distance. He calls, "water-r-r-r." Gradually he crawls on stage, dragging himself.When he reaches the water hole he takes a dipper, drinks the water, spits out some, screams "POISON!" and drops.

The bucket has a little rice or confetti in the bottom and some water in the dipper, which is carefully replaced.

Other prospectors come in and drink, with the same results, each screaming "POISON!" and dropping. When the last one is just about to drink, the first one, supposedly dead, springs up and screams, "DON'T DRINK THAT WATER, IT'S POISON!" and grabs the bucket, hurling the contents out over the audience, who know that there is water in the dipper, and expect a bucketful on them!

(NOTE: for a build-up, an announcer could carefully explain about the problem of finding suitable water on the desert and spin a yarn about an experience of his. Also, a recording of the Sons of the Pioneers quartet, called "Water!" would bring in good atmosphere.)

Little Shot[24]

SCENE: *A grocery store. Older man for storekeeper.*

At the outset he mutters to himself, "This lumbago is jist

[23] From Buford and Betty Bush, Inverness, Calif.
[24] *Ibid.*

about a-killin' me. I shure wish I felt like I did when I was twenty-five! Well, guess I'd better straighten up. Here's some B-B shot. Kids jist don't buy 'em the way they used to. I'll put 'em up on the top shelf! *(Gets a ladder and painfully climbs to top shelf. If no shelf is available, he might leave them on top of the stepladder.)*

When he is finished, a boy comes in and wants to buy a nickel's worth of B-B's. The storekeeper climbs up the ladder painfully, climbs down again, sells to boy. A second boy comes in, wants some shot, so he clambers up again and gets the shot for the boy, comes down again, muttering to himself, and takes the money.

A third boy comes in. He looks at him and says, "Never mind, son, I know what *you* want," and climbs up for the third time, gets a package, brings it down, hands it to the boy. Boy is not completely pleased.

"Ain't that what you wanted, son?" asks the storekeeper.

"Sure, Mister Aiken," says the boy. "But I wanted *two* packages!"

Storekeeper faints.

Thought Waves[25]

The two "operators" indicate that they can pass numbers on to each other by mental telepathy.

Anyone from the audience may come up and write a number on the board. Then the assistant will speak to the Master Mind, who will immediately give out the number written.

Someone comes forward and writes, "4," whereupon the assistant gives the Master Mind four slaps on the back (with conversation to cover up) and he says, "Four."

Another comes up and writes "2" with the same result.

A stooge from the audience comes forward and writes, "00." The assistant looks very puzzled and doesn't seem to

[25] *Ibid.*

know what to say. Then he "kicks" the Master Mind on the shins and makes some wild motions and the Master Mind says, "00"! (Oh! Oh!)

The Paper Read Aloud

Three or four persons are sitting on the stage or are observed, reading the paper. One snickers, starts to tell a joke. Another interrupts, reading from the gossip column (some local news), and another begins to tell about a bargain he saw in the paper. They read louder and talk louder. Finally they all leave in a huff, glaring at each other. Then the joke teller returns and finishes telling his joke. *(It should be a good one.)*

Sweet Mystery[26]

SCENE: *Somewhere in an army camp. Sergeant, Mrs. Gushalot, men.*

NARRATOR: My friends, we bring you this story for whatever it is worth. We cannot absolutely vouch for its accuracy, but we think you will be interested because it was such a long, valiant search that Mrs. Gushalot carried on in order that she might thank personally one who had done her such a great favor. And here is our sketch. We hope you like it.

MRS. GUSHALOT: Oh, sergeant, I know I am not supposed to be here . . .

SERGEANT: No, lady, you ain't.

MRS. G: But I'm on an unusual mission and need your help.

SERGEANT: What is it, lady?

MRS. G: You know about Mr. Rhee, of Korea?

SERGEANT: Sure.

MRS. G: Do you know that his son is a photographer for *Life* Magazine?

[26] From Bill Wilson, Birmingham, Ala.

SERGEANT *(impatiently)*: Naw.

MRS. G: Well, he is . . . and he is the sweetest thing. He did me the most wonderful favor, and I want to repay him! I've heard he's here.

SERGEANT: Now that you mention it, I think he *is* here.

MRS. G: Oh, if I could only see him. I want to thank him and give him something of my appreciation.

SERGEANT: Sure, ma'am. Come with me.

MRS. G. *(looking off stage at the supposed Mr. Rhee, Junior)*: There he is. There he is. Ah, sweet, Mr. Rhee, of *Life*, at *last* I've found thee!"

Rubber

A baby has been left in his carriage outside a store. Two persons of great dignity of speech and position are viewing it.

FIRST: I say, Smithkins, what a baby!

SECOND: Tomkins, you are right. *What* a baby!

FIRST: It looks like my Aunt Agatha!

SECOND: In truth, it does.

FIRST: And I always thought Aunt Agatha was the ugliest woman I ever saw.

SECOND: There's no disputing!

Both are staring at the child in fascinated horror when its mother comes out. She sees them, and with strong feeling, utters the single word, "RUBBER!" contemptuously at both of them and leaves.

FIRST *(to Second, after a pause)*: Thank heavens, what a relief. I was thinking it might be real!

Bum's Rush

LEADER: Friends, we want to give you a little skit here now. It just involves two of our number, but we thought you would enjoy it. One of the characters could be called a "panhandler." I have a cousin who is a panhandler—he is an intern over at the local hospital. But *this man* is just a bum. As our scene opens, he approaches another man on the street:

BUM: Say, mister, could I have a moment of your time?
MAN: What do you want with it?
BUM: Would you gimme two bits for a bed?
MAN: Hummmmm! Maybe. Let's see the bed first!

Bum looks at him peculiarly and walks off. Man grins, walks on down the street.

Letter Carrier[27]

SCENE: *The prison. Two prisoners are seen at opposite sides of the stage. Each of them has on striped clothes. They have their heads down and only speak to each other as they pass.*

"Hey."
"Hey."
"Who are you?"
"Slug. Who're you?"
"Blackie."
"How long you in?"
"Life. How long for you?"
"Twenty years."
"Do something for me?"
"Depends."
"No trouble."
"O K . . . what?"
"Mail this letter when you get out."

Ticket, Please[28]

SCENE: *A railroad station. The gawky daughter sits over in*

[27] From Buford and Betty Bush, Inverness, Calif.
[28] *Ibid.*

the waiting room, her mother approaches the ticket window.

MAW: Hey, mister?

AGENT: Yes, ma'am.

MAW: This whurr you sell tickets?

AGENT: Certainly.

MAW: Gimme a ticket fer Magnolia.

AGENT: Just a minute. *(Starts looking through his timetables and books. Can't find it.)* Would you repeat that, please?

MAW: Certainly. I ast ye fer a ticket fer Magnolia.

Agent shakes his head, starts back through all of it again. Mutters to himself and gets more and more exasperated.

AGENT: Lady, I wonder if you would tell me where Magnolia is?

MAW: Sure. 'Course I can. Tharr she sets, right over tharr.
Agent faints.

The Mirror[29]

SCENE: *The mountains. A tourist has gone and left a mirror, which the members of the family have never seen before.*

Paw discovers it on the ground. He looks in it, runs away. Props it up, comes up to it again. Thinks it's another man. Calls Maw. She comes and looks into it. Decides that it is a woman that Paw has been running around with, and cuffs him a few times, just to be on the safe side.

Sons and daughters of various sizes and ages come and look into the contraption, with many remarks about the appearance of the one they see in the mirror.

The ending is varied. The mirror may get broken. Somebody may come to claim it, telling what it is. Or one of the family may say, "Shore am glad our family ain't as ugly as the one in that contraption."

[29] From Mary Alice Oliver, Scarritt College, Nashville, Tenn.

Family Album

MOTHER *(sits reading a book when a knock is heard):* Come in.

SON: Mother, I always told you someday I'd bring home the girl that I would marry. Well, I've found her at last and I want you to meet Cynthia Kate.

MOTHER: Well, welcome, Cynthia Kate. It is surely nice to have you in our home, and I'm sure you must be hungry so if you'll excuse me I'll run out to the kitchen and get a bite of supper. John, why don't you entertain Cynthia Kate by showing her some of the family pictures in the album. If I do say it myself, as I shouldn't, we come from a fine-looking family.

CYNTHIA KATE: Oh, that's very nice of you to invite me for supper, and I just can't think of anything as exciting as looking at family pictures.

JOHN: Well, here they are, honey. How do you like this one?

CYNTHIA KATE: It's very interesting. I suppose that this is one of your uncles. Does he raise these sheep dogs as pets or for sale?

JOHN: Shucks, those aren't sheep dogs! That's Aunt Mehitabel and their twins with him.

CYNTHIA KATE: I'm so sorry! Here is an interesting candid shot of someone at the breakfast table, looking over a stack of buckwheat cakes.

JOHN: Wrong again, my sweet, that's Grandfather. He had the finest set of double chins you ever saw. *(Aside.* Now here is one of father and me when I was a lad. This will surely wow her.) Now, Cynthia Kate, here is one I'm sure you'll like.

CYNTHIA KATE: Oh, it is an interesting picture. Who is this fine-looking man?

JOHN: That's my father.

CYNTHIA KATE: How clever he must be. Was he in vaudeville?

JOHN: No, what made you say that?

CYNTHIA KATE: I thought he must be a ventriloquist, with that ridiculous dummy on his knee.

Peanut Butter

SCENE: *Noontime at a work project, with several workmen eating lunches.*

SCENE I

Our hero takes out his lunch kit, looks through it carefully, takes out a sandwich, unwraps the waxed paper, looks into it, scowls, growls, "Peanut butter!" and throws away the sandwich violently. Other workmen look on puzzled, as he stalks off.

SCENE II

Next day our hero smiles, goes through the same procedure exactly.

SCENE III

Procedure is the same, but one of his workmen friends stops him as he begins to stalk away and says, "I don't want to butt into your business, buddy, but . . . why don't you tell your wife you don't like peanut butter sandwiches?"

To which our hero replies, "You leave my wife out of this. I make my *own* sandwiches."

Bills Lost

SCENE: *A bank. Several customers are there doing business with the tellers.*

OLD GENTLEMAN: I wish I thought people were as honest as they used to be.

MAN: They are. I don't think there's any difference these days.

OLD MAN: Well, you may be right, but I have my doubts. It

used to be that you could take a man's word in business. Now we don't do that.

MAN: That's true— but it's better to have business deals in writing.

OLD MAN: I suppose so. Just look around at the people here. How many of them could you trust?

MAN: Why, most of them, I believe.

OLD MAN: Well, let's just try an experiment and see.

Whispers into man's ear. He grins, agrees.

OLD MAN *(in loud voice):* I say, did anybody here lose a small roll of bills with a rubber band around it?

VOICES *(several customers):* Yes! I did. It's mine!

OLD MAN: Well, I just wanted to say that I have the rubber band here!

Picks it up from the floor, holds it up for. . . .

BLACKOUT

Court Scene

SCENE: *A court room.*

CHARACTERS: *A judge, two attorneys, court officer, spectators if desired, and three others.*

COURT OFFICER: Silence in the court! The session is about to begin.

JUDGE: Are all the news cameramen here?

OFFICER: Yes, your honor!

JUDGE: Lights OK?

OFFICER: Yes, your honor.

JUDGE: Sound?

OFFICER: OK, your honor!

JUDGE: Good! Then let justice roll. Whose is the first case?

OFFICER: Jonathan Meekly, your honor. He wants a divorce.

JUDGE: Bring him in. *(Officer does so.)* You are Jonathan Meekly?

MEEKLY: Yes, your honor.

JUDGE: And you want to part from your wife?

MEEKLY: Yes, your honor.

JUDGE: What are the causes?

MEEKLY: She treats me mean and inhuman, Judge. She hits me with things.

JUDGE: Such as . . . ?

MEEKLY: Well, Judge, just the other day she hit me with an oak leaf!

JUDGE: Why, I don't think that is so bad. It was probably just a . . . love tap. It couldn't really hurt!

MEEKLY: Oh, couldn't it? It was the oak leaf from the center of the dining room table!

JUDGE: In that case, plea granted. Next case.

OFFICER: Farmer Benjamin Sturdley versus Slick McGlick, your honor.

JUDGE: What are the charges?

OFFICER: Hunting on the property of Mr. Sturdley without permission!

JUDGE: Call Farmer Sturdley. Is Mr. McGlick's lawyer ready?

UNDERWOOD: Yes, your honor. *(Turns to Farmer.)* When do you say this trespassing took place?

FARMER: I think . . .

UNDERWOOD *(snaps):* We don't care what you think, sir. We must know what you know!

FARMER: Then I can't testify, I reckon. Not being a lawyer, I don't believe I can talk without thinking!

UNDERWOOD: Are you prepared to swear that Mr. McGlick shot your pigeons?

FARMER: I didn't exactly say he shot 'em. I said I suspected it.

UNDERWOOD: Well, what made you suspect it?

FARMER: Well, I caught him on my land with a gun. I heard a gun go off and saw some pigeons fall. Then I found four of my pigeons in his pocket. I just don't believe they committed suicide!

JUDGE: Call the prisoner. In the light of this evidence, McGlick, I'll give you 10 days or $20.

McGLICK: I'll just take the $20 and thanks, Judge.

JUDGE: Are you trying to show contempt for this court?

McGLICK: No, your honor. I'm trying to conceal it. I'd like to ask one request, Judge.

JUDGE: Quick! What is it?

McGLICK: Give me a sentence with the word freedom in it.

JUDGE: All right. You can have your freedom in ten days.

BLACKOUT

Bashful Lover

SCENE: *The beach. He and She are alone. Play it slow, with pauses.*

SHE: Reginald, this is so lovely here at the beach.

HE: Lovely!

SHE: Darling, do you think of me a lot?

HE: Sure.

SHE: Am I in your thoughts and affections all the time?

HE: All the time.

SHE: Do you think I am prettier than any of the other girls here at the resort?

HE: Yes.

SHE: Oh, Reginald . . . . . . , you say the most lovely things!

Silence. She becomes more cozy, her head on his shoulder, etc.

SHE: Reggie?

HE: Yes?

SHE: Why don't you kiss me?

HE: I can't.

SHE: Why, darling?

HE: Got some sand in my mouth a while ago.

SHE: Swallow it, Reggie, swallow it.

HE: Why, darling?

SHE: If there ever was a boy who needed a little sand, you certainly are the one!

BLACKOUT

Crimebusters

While the party is going strong, or a meeting or conference or banquet is in progress, several people, coached previously, rush in, enact a crime quickly before the group, and leave.

Quickly it is decided to have a trial, or at least an investigation. Several persons are called to the witness stand to give details of the crime as they remember them. FBI, police inspectors, dragnets, and other terms may flow freely.

Mother

SCENE: *A home where husband and wife are talking. A little old lady may be rocking, knitting, as the two talk in low tones.*

JOHN: Ethel, dear?

ETHEL: Yes?

JOHN: There's something I wanted to talk with you about.

ETHEL: What's that, darling?

JOHN: It's about . . . mother.

ETHEL *(looking toward the little old lady):* Yes . . . mother.

JOHN: Really, I don't want to be too harsh, but she has been with us for fifteen years now.

ETHEL *(puzzled):* Yes, that's right.

JOHN: And I think it's about time that your mother got an apartment of her own.

ETHEL *(shocked, astounded): My* mother! I thought she was *your* mother!

Shake Well!

Two persons are talking; one is shaking all over.

FIRST: What's the matter with you?
SECOND: I've got to take my medicine as soon as this is over.
FIRST: Well, what's the matter?
SECOND: You see that bottle?
FIRST: Yeah!
SECOND: It says, "Shake well before taking!"

chapter 4

THESE
GROUP
STUNTS
NEED A
NARRATOR

THESE GROUP STUNTS NEED A NARRATOR

HERE ARE included several skits and ideas for skits involving the use of a narrator. Most of them require little rehearsal. In the case of "Combing the Air Waves," a combination of the commercials and perhaps the sketches might be made to advantage. A few other "narrator" skits, shorter than the ones included here, appeared in Chapter 2.

Cave Man Stuff

The narrator reads, the actors act them out. The cast includes papa and mama Neanderthal, daughter Tibia, Willie her boy friend, and Hairy the villain. Imagination may be used to concoct their costumes, the opening of the cave in the background, and other features. A rhythmic tapping in the background may be used for the strong beats.

NARRATOR

Here is a story you will like.
　　The time: before Pike's Peak was Pike . . .
Back in the days when we lived in caves,
And raw meat stews brought on the raves.

There was a couple, brown and tan,
　　Neanderthal woman and Neanderthal man;　*Ma and Pa*
They lived in a cave over by the river.　*appear on the*
　　(The cave was the best that he could give　*scene.*
　　her.)

They had a daughter, and oh, my gracious,　*Daughter*
　　That little cave gal was really curvacious!　*makes her*
Many a cave boy longed to dare　*appearance.*
　　To take her to a cave home by the hair!

She loved a boy whose name was Willie,
   Pop and Mom thought him just too silly.
"He's just too young, and he's not too strong,
   What if a cave bully came along?"

Willie flirts
with
daughter.

That's just what papa always said,
   Nights before Maw went to bed.
"I want her a man with a hairy chest,
   Not a weak little runt like that, the pest!"

Paw lays
down the law
as Maw
combs hair
with fishbone
comb.

And so things went along, day by day;
   Our heroine, Tibia, liked to play,
And play she did, in the country hilly,
   With her little cave lover, her "silly Willie."

They play
Hide and
Seek behind
trees.

Then, one day, there came right along,
   A hairy-chested bully with a club that would
      bong
Any cave person who didn't please him!
   And the girls . . . he tried to squeeze 'em!

Tough, hairy
character
comes in with
club. Chases
girls.

He made the cave people bring him food,
   This they did till they were all poohed!
Tired of this, when he called for venison,
   The people got together and they said in
      unison:

People bring
food. They
are tired.

"We've had enough of this here tyrant!
   Let's go swear out a great big wirrant!"
"All very well, he does deserve it,
   But who in the dickens is gonna serve it?"

Pantomine
unrest and
these
statements.

The people cried out, with one big tear-o,
   "What we need is a great big hero."

"Hairy" went to Neanderthal home,
  In his hand he carried a pome: *Arrives,*
"Here's what I want, I will not fib-ya   *shows poem*
  I'm gonna take your daughter, Tibia!   *to papa.*
By the strength of the hair that's on my chest— *Tibia hears.*
  The best man win! (And I'm the best!)"

Tibia screamed as she ran into the cave,   *Tibia screams*
  This just made old Hairy rave,   *and runs,*
"Come on, gal, before I'm mad,   *Hairy behind*
  When I'm mad I'm *really* bad!"   *her.*

Now appeared in the door our Willie.   *Willie*
  Gone was the air of the lad that was silly!   *appears.*
                                               Looks manly.

"Hairy, I don't like a fuss,   *Willy talks*
  Cave's too little for both of us.   *like a tough*
Do you want that I should hit-zu,   *hombre.*
  Or would you prefer I use Jiu-jitsu?"

Hairy roared (the great big boob)   *If some sort*
  But Willy squirted him with hair-remover   *of false hair*
    tube!   *and wigs can*
The lotion made him peel off all his hair,   *be used, so*
  Head and chest were mighty bare!   *much the*
                                                   better.

Hairy moaned with head in hand,
  "This is what made me a man!"   *Suits action*
Hair was what he valued most . . . so   *to words.*
  Seeing where he was, he gave up the ghost!

Tibia fell in the arms of Willy.
  (She'd never said that he was silly!)   *Suit action to*
Then he whispered, "Tibia, let's elope!   *words.*
  I've got a ladder right down the slope."

Tibia was willing, then and there,   *Takes her by*
  So he grabbed her by the hair,   *hair, goes*
Carried her right down the ladder.   *down ladder*
  (This made Tibia gladder and gladder.)   *if one can be*
                                                     arranged.

Maw said, "Hey, Neanderthal man,   *Maw points*
  Come right here as quick as you can.   *out action to*
That boy's doing just like he oughter,   *Paw.*
  He's eloping with our beautiful daughter!"

Paw just looked and said, "I'm willin',   *Paw blesses*
  Blessings on both of you, my chillin!   *them.*
Always said that boy was a prize!"   *Maw looks*
  Maw said nothing, but just looked wise.   *wise.*

Willie wed Tibia, and how he kissed her,   *Suit action to*
  Now that they were Mrs. and Mr.   *words,*
Since it's known she had no sister,   *burlesque.*
  Thus ends the story of your ancestor.

The Chartreuse Murder Case

This is one of those stunts that calls for the advance preparation of many signs and properties, but otherwise is easy to do, since the narrator reads, and the actors act out what he has read. One rehearsal will be needed, and more may help to smooth the performance, but would not be absolutely necessary.

If some of the properties are too hard to get, just read the line and drop the action, or drop both line and action. The story will probably not be greatly affected.

As soon as the forest lines have been given, the trees may leave, so that the stage will be free for the other actors.

SETTING: *Part of the stage has trees on it, part represents the inside of Lord Beaverbottom's residence. The only neces-*

sary furniture includes a chair (for Lord Beaverbottom) two tables (to get turned later).

For easy staging, it might be good to have a third table (or use one of the turned tables) on which to place the properties. In the room are needed:

1. *Alarm clock works in Lord B's chair, light with bulb to be unscrewed.*

2. *A hammer in or near the chair, also false face.*

3. *Bubble gum or bills with hole punched through, for "shot wad," in or near the chair.*

4. *Signs: "HORRD FASCNATION" near the chair. "THE SITUATION," "WORK," "THE STAIRS," "ON" and "OFF," and "SUSPICION."*
   The butler sees the sign, "THE SITUATION." He knocks off "WORK." Lady Beaverbottom then tears down "THE STAIRS." The detective takes "OFF." "SUSPICION" hangs over the lovers, or is held by a person over their heads from behind.

5. *Other signs: "SCENE," "HARDWOOD TREE" (several), "SOFTWOOD TREE" (several). "THUN-DER," "LIGHTNING," "MOON," "THE CHANCE" (the latter for the detective).*

6. *Properties needed. For "THUNDER," potlids. For "LIGHTNING," a flashlight. For "MOON," a loaded cap pistol. For niece, a crayon (for finishing sign), chalk, red cardboard tulips. For detective, tape measure, sign "THE CHANCE." For Sir Loin, sign materials, an iron. For butler, plate and scraper. For Lady B, postage stamp. For Lord B, cardboard heel on his back and/or beaver tail.*

NARRATOR	ACTION
Our scene is laid in the Black Forest.	*A person with SCENE on a sign is laid in the "forest."*
Here we find some of those wonderful hardwood trees.	*Narrator checks them by knocking on them.*
And soft woods, too!	*Narrator checks; soft woods are much softer.*
It is raining cats and dogs.	*People on all fours, meowing and barking, roam the forest.*
The thunder crashes and roars.	*Person with sign THUNDER crashes pot lids, roars.*
Lightning flashes among the trees.	*Person with sign LIGHT-NING flashes light among the trees.*
The scene is at Chartreuse Castle, the time is midnight.	*Clock strikes fifteen times. Narrator counts to twelve, then says: "12:01, 12:02, 12:03. It is just past midnight."*
The world-famous detective, Spurlock Homes (not to be confused with a subdivision of the same name) has sensed that something might be cooking over at Chartreuse Manor! He creeps in stealthily.	*Detective creeps in, sniffs, nods knowingly.*
What he sees there leaves him GLUED TO THE SPOT.	*He tries to lift feet, can't.*
Inside, he sees Lord Beaverbottom on his last legs, sinking into a chair.	*Over to the right of the stage, Lord Beaverbottom sinks into a chair.*
"Someone has given him the works," says the famous detective.	*He goes over, lifts an old alarm clock to show audience.*

NARRATOR	ACTION
"I believe he has lost heart."	*Picks up a tremendous red valentine.*
"Yes, I am almost sure of it. Every evidence points to the fact that he has kicked the bucket."	*Picks up a bucket. (If a dent is in the side of it, it will look as if bucket has been kicked.)*
Here the detective's sharp eyes dart around the room.	*Picks up darts marked EYES and tosses two or three.*
"Aha!" says he triumphantly as he sees a clue, and he makes a MENTAL NOTE of it.	*Writes on his forehead.*
Just then the clock strikes.	*Sound of heavy object striking the floor (perhaps with glass tinkling).*
The moon rises and shoots eerie beams around the room.	*Person with sign MOON rises, shoots beams with cap pistol.*
Then the doors fly open	*Persons with signs DOORS "fly" open, making flying motions with hands.*
and in sweeps Lord Beaverbottom's lovely niece.	*She is sweeping with a broom.*
Her train she carries daintily behind her.	*Toy train, on a string or pinned behind her. She must turn so audience can see.*
"Oh!" she gasps, and fixes her eyes in horrid fascination on Lord Beaverbottom.	*She takes a sign which says, "HORR D FASC NATION" and fixes the i's with a crayon, lays it on him. Backs up.*

NARRATOR	ACTION
Turning to the great detective, she says, "He's gone?" The great detective measures a glance at the silent figure and NOTES his height. "Long gone," he answers.	*Detective measures a glance with tape measure. Makes note of his height.*
She crosses the floor once again to where her uncle sits in the chair.	*Makes "X's" with chalk.*
"He has been seen gamboling on the green," she says. "He lost heavily—55 pounds. Perhaps it is just that he could not stand to lose face."	*Reaches down into his chair and brings up a false face.*
Just then her lover, Sir Loin, makes his QUICK APPEARANCE.	*He rushes in, makes a sign, "QUICK APPEARANCE."*
Behind is the butler, bowing and scraping.	*Butler has a plate that he is scraping for washing as he bows.*
Seeing "THE SITUATION," the Butler knocks off WORK.	*He sees a sign saying, "THE SITUATION" and knocks off a table a person bearing sign WORK.*
"Who is responsible for this heartless situation?" cries Sir Loin. "The thing is grave enough," says the great detective. "Butler, what do you know about this?"	
"Sir," says the butler, "Lord Beaverbottom may have knocked himself out."	*Holds up a hammer near the chair.*

NARRATOR	ACTION
"Ah," says Spurlock Homes, "it seems that he has shot his wad."	*Holds up huge piece of bubble gum with hole through it or dollar bills, if more convenient.*
The two lovers look at each other. "Are we under SUSPICION?" they ask.	*Person holds a sign SUSPICION over their heads from behind; or it can be suspended from ceiling.*
"You are not above suspicion," says the great detective.	
"Have no fear," says Sir Loin, as he presses his lady's hand.	*Presses it with an iron.*
"Soon the tables will be turned."	*Turns two small tables.*
Just then Lady Beaverbottom comes tearing down THE STAIRS.	*Tears down a sign THE STAIRS.*
She blows into the room for she feels that she is being egged on by someone.	*Blows.* *Someone behind her is throwing eggshells at her. (Blow out the insides or just use shells.)*
Then her eyes fall on Lord Beaverbottom.	*She lets two cardboard eyes fall on him.*
"May I give *you* the chance to solve this mystery?" says the great detective.	*Holds out a large card with "THE CHANCE."*
She jumps at THE CHANCE, and begins to talk a blue streak.	*Does so.* *Pulls blue ribbon out of mouth as she talks.*
"Lord Beaverbottom . . ." she shrieks at him, and stamps his foot.	*Pastes a stamp on his foot. (If you prefer, stamp hers.)*

"Snap out of it."

He jumps suddenly from the chair and looks around.

"You come with me, you heel," she says, whisking him from the room.

Optional gags: have a heel on his back (large cardboard), also possibly a beaver tail for "Lord Beaverbottom." She uses a whiskbroom to get him from the room.

The young lovers are overjoyed. They dance around the room. "Then we are no longer under suspicion?" asks Sir Loin.

They dance around.

"No, it is no longer hanging over you," answers the detective.

The sign SUSPICION drops.

"You may take OFF when you please."

There are two signs ON and OFF, perhaps over a light.

"On second thought, perhaps I should take OFF."

He takes the "Off" sign and leaves.

The lovers are alone. Sir Loin feels that he should press his suit.

Takes the iron, takes off his coat, and starts pressing.

So he turns to his lovely companion and pleads, "Will you give me your lovely red tulips?"

She gives him a couple of cardboard tulips.

He sighs with rapture. "Ah-h-h-h . . . in this I really take delight."

Unscrews light globe and takes it.

"Come and fly around the globe with me," he says.

He puts bulb on ground, they fly around it.

"What a wonderful trip," she says.

She is tripped as she flies around the globe. They leave.

And then, dear friends as in all stories like this, they get married, get kids, get fat, and live happily ever after—more or less.

Narrator bows, turns, shows a sign on the back of his coat, "The End," as he leaves.

Teaching Them to Drive[1]

The lines of this skit are such that they may be memorized by the "husband" and the "lover," read by them, or read by two extra persons. Place two chairs at the right of the stage for the "husband and his wife" and two chairs at the left for the "lover and his sweetheart." The husband first gives his wife the instructions in verse No. 1; then the lover gives the instructions in verse No. 2. They alternate in the order of the verse numbers. Avoid kissing by lowering in front of the sweethearts a placard on which "SMACK" is written and by making an appropriate noise backstage.

HUSBAND TO HIS WIFE	LOVER TO HIS SWEETHEART
1. First, you see your car is out of gear. How? By this gearshift lever here. How can you tell? Well, feel it. See? The thing is simple as can be.	2. To learn to drive the auto, dear, First put the lever into gear, Then push your left foot in like this. That's fine. Now, teacher gets a kiss.

[1] From *Stunts and Skits,* compiled by F. L. McReynolds.

3. Now step on that to make it start.
Great Scott! You'll tear it all apart
If you don't take your foot off quick
The second that it gives a kick!

4. Now step upon the starter, so.
That makes the precious engine go.
Now let your left foot back like this.
Good! Teacher gets another kiss.

5. Now throw your clutch. For goodness sake!
Your clutch! Your clutch! No, not your brake!
Why? 'Cause I tell you to, that's why.
There, now, you needn't start to cry.

6. Upon the gas you now must step.
That fills the engine full of pep.
That's great! You are a clever miss.
Here, teacher gets another kiss.

7. Now pull this lever into low.
Step on the gas and start off slow.
Look out! You almost hit the fence.
Here, let me drive. You've got no sense!

8. Now change to second. Now to high.
You can do it just as well as I.
Now stop the car right here, and then,
We'll do the lesson once again.

Lochinvar

By Sir Walter Scott

NARRATOR (reads)

Oh, young Lochinvar is come out of the west
Through all the wide border his steed was the best;
And save his good broadsword

NOTES

Lochinvar is riding a stick horse. He draws up his animal (which may have an improvised head) and puts his hand to his side, where there

he weapons had none,
He rode all unarmed, and he rode all alone
So faithful in love, and so dauntless in war
There never was knight like the young Lochinvar.

is a tremendous cardboard sword.

He staid not for break, and he stopped not for stone
He swam the Eske River where ford there was none.
But 'ere he alighted at Netherby gate
The bride has consented. The gallant came late.
For a laggard in love, and a dastard in war
Was to wed the fair Ellen of brave Lochinvar.

He rides hard (perhaps through the audience to give more space), acts as if he and steed are fording the river, arrives at Netherby Hall, which may be on the stage, labeled by a sign.

So boldly he entered the Netherby Hall
Among the bridesman, and kinsmen, and brothers, and all
Then spoke the bride's father, his hand on his sword,
For the poor craven bridegroom said never a word,
"Oh! come ye in peace here, or come ye in war
Or to dance at our bridal, young Lord Lochinvar?"

He strides into the Hall, full of manly vigor and disdain. The father and the sniveling bridegroom are much in evidence, and act their parts as directed. Lochinvar approaches his host. Is questioned.

"I long wooed your daughter, my suit you denied;

He speaks poetically, with motions.

Love swells like the Solway,
    but ebbs like its tide;
And now am I come with this
    lost love of mine
To lead but one measure,
    drink one cup of wine.
There are maidens in Scot-
    land more lovely by far
That would gladly be bride to
    the young Lochinvar."

The bride kissed the goblet;   *Suit actions to the descrip-*
    the knight took it up   *tion.*
He quaffed off the wine, and
    he threw down the cup.
She looked down to blush,
    and she looked up to sigh
With a smile on her lips, and
    a tear in her eye.
He took her soft hand, ere her
    mother could bar.
"Now tread we a measure,"
    said the young Lochinvar.

So stately his form, and so   *Here they tread a measure,*
    lovely her face,   *the others act their parts as*
That never a hall such a gal-   *described.*
    lard did grace
While her mother did fret,
    and her father did fume
And the bridegroom stood
    dangling his bonnet and
    plume;
And the bridemaidens
    whispered, "It were better
    by far,

To have matched our fair
    cousin with young Lochin-
    var."

One touch to her hand, and
    one word in her ear
When they reached the hall
    door, and the charger stood
    near;
So light to the croupe the fair
    lady he swung,
So light to the saddle before
    her he sprung!
"She is won! We are gone,
    over bank, bush, and scaur;
They'll have fleet steeds that
    follow," quoth young Loch-
    invar.

*Here he makes off with her
on his "charger." They mount
the stick horse and ride away.
Lochinvar makes dramatic
motions to go with his
speeches.*

There was mounting 'mong
    Graemes of the Netherby
    clan;
Forsters, Fenwicks, and Mus-
    graves, they rode and they
    ran,
There was racing and chasing
    on Cannobie Lea
But the lost bride of Netherby
    ne'er did they see.
So daring in love and so
    dauntless in war,
Have ye e'er heard of gallant
    like young Lochinvar?

*They give chase, but he gets
away (through the audience
if convenient).*

The Eskimo Tragedy[2]

SCENE

North Pole *(boy enters carrying huge pole labeled North Pole)*

Icebergs *(several persons draped in white sheets labeled icebergs)*

Footlights *(two or more persons lying on back holding flashlights in feet up in air)*

Wind howling *(several persons offstage howling weirdly)*

Snow blowing *(handfuls of torn paper thrown around or blown by electric fan)*

CAST

Eskimo, Eskimaid, Fido the dog *(dog carries huge sign reading FIDO)*, Eskimucker, Eskimoon

NARRATOR *(reads):*

Mid Greenland's polar ice and snow	*Eskimo enters appropriately clad.*
Where watermelons seldom grow,	
It's far too cold up there you know—	
There lived a bold young Eskimo.	
Beneath the selfsame iceberg's shade,	*Eskimaid minces on, appropriately clad.*
In fur of bear and seal arrayed	
Not overcleanly, I'm afraid,	
There lived a charming Eskimaid.	

[2] From *Ice Breakers and the Ice Breaker Herself,* Edna Geister (New York: Harper and Brothers, 1930).

Throughout the six months' night they'd spoon
O, ye in love, think what a boon!
To stop at ten is far too soon
Beneath the silvery Eskimoon.

(rub large wooden spoons together)—
Moon comes on—huge disc labeled MOON carried by some person.

The hated rival now we see,
You spy the coming tragedy—
But I can't help it, don't blame me—
An Eskimucker vile is he.

Eskimucker comes in, dressed in villain style.

He spies the fond pair there alone,
And kills them with his axi-bone.
You see how fierce the tale has grown—
The fond pair dies with an Eskimoan.

Eskimaid and Eskimo die with groans and moans. Here's a good place to really ham it up.

Two graves were dug deep in the ice
And lined with fur, fishheads, and spice.
The two were buried in a trice.
Quite safe from all the Eskimice.

Several little Eskimice, labeled, can frisk on and off the stage at this point.

Now Fido comes. Alas, too late—
I hope it's not too indelicate
These little incidents to state—
The Eskimucker, he promptly ate.

Fido eats Eskimucker with much growling and lots of yelling from Eskimucker.

Upon an Eskimo to sup   *Dog dies here.*
Was much too much for an
  Eskipup
He died, also, ere the sun
  came up.

Schmikel Hair Tonic[3]

This series of commercials would, of course, be spaced out with some acts, music, and skits in between. Other gags about hair tonic might be added.

ANNOUNCER: And now, Station FMFM and FMFM-FM bring you the Schmikel Hair Tonic Show. Ladies and gentlemen, hair tonic is sold in bottles, tubes, cans, boxes, and drugstores . . . but the new Schmikel is an entirely different kind of hair tonic. The new Schmikel is frozen on a stick. Yes, the SCHMIKEL SICLE has what it takes to fix up your hair. Go to your nearest frozen food store and buy a stick of Schmikel—today!

Music or a Skit

ANNOUNCER: Mothers, do you have children . . . children with untrained hair? Then you will find the new Schmikel a boon for you. Schmikel trains the hair. Yes, Schmikel can train the hair to lie down, sit up, roll over, or play dead. Mothers with little boys, the new SCHMIKEL SICLE is *the* tonic for your *heirs!*

More Music or Skits

ANNOUNCER: We address this to those men who must comb their hair with a washrag. Schmikel offers you new hope in the SCHMIKEL SICLE. It makes your hair come in, and it makes your hair come in heavy. We guarantee this. Listen to this testimonial by Mr. I. B. Slick. This is the voice of Mr. Slick.

[3] From Charles Broyles, Jackson, Miss.

Voice: Schmikel made my hair come in heavy. I have only one hair, but it weighs eighteen pounds!

More Music or Skits

Announcer: If you were surprised at the testimony of Mr. Slick about Schmikel you will be amazed at this true-to-life conversation. Listen.

Voice: Mac, *you've* got hair.

Second: Yes, I know. I've been using the new SCHMIKEL SICLE.

Voice: And Schmikel turned your shining dome into a hay-loft?

Second Voice: Man, Schmikel will grow hair on a billiard ball.

Voice: Will, huh? Yes, but doesn't that ruin your game?

Announcer: This program has come to you over the facilities of the Miracle Broadcasting Company. If it's a good program, it's a Miracle.

Combing the Air Waves[4]

Here are some good-humored laughs at radio and TV, especially about the products that they eulogize. Put together your own combination, of course, and get some fresh angles by listening and viewing, yourself. These are merely samples. Two or more announcers may be used, and some of these sketches will call for several voices.

Voice 1: If you think you are well and hearty,
       Go over (if you feel brave)
       And turn on the TV or radio
       While the advertisers rave.

[4] This section is compiled from contributions from Robert Blount, Jr., Gainesville, Texas; Bill Wilson, Birmingham, Ala.; Martha Jane Koestline, Hammond, Ind., and Sibley C. Burnett, Nashville, Tenn.

VOICE 2: Don't wait until you have a headache. Ask for one today.

VOICE 1: Their manner is certain, their science is slick,
And soon you'll be feeling quite shaky and sick.
Take this or take that, rush right out and buy,
If you don't get so-so you're ready to die.

VOICE 2: Have you tried the new Lost? It is a product of the Thrivo Company. If your liver quivers, or if your lung is sprung, why don't you get LOST!

VOICE 1: Now mother's delight and father's bore
Are found in the soap opera serials galore,
Mother is terrified daily to hear
That John's other wife is not with him this year.

VOICE 2: *(Improvises a soap opera plot.)*

VOICE 1: For the cultured in taste, the discriminating wife
Who loves the aesthetic things of life,
For those who belong to the metropolitan set,
We proudly present that classic of all . . . SHRIMPNET.
The story you are about to see and hear is true. Only the faces have been changed to protect the audience.

VOICE 2: 7:47 P.M., Tuesday, July 8. It was snowing in Los Angeles. We were working day watch out of night detail. My partner's name is Sam Ketcham St. George. The Boss is Captain Marvelous. My car is a '36 Blue Plymouth with seven carburetors and a jacked up rear end. I use Red H Gasoline. My name is Thursday. A boy has been missing from his home for ten years. He was last seen going to the store for a loaf of bread and the _____ (local newspaper). His parents were beginning to worry. Their hunger for supper aroused suspicion. . . . (Etc.)

VOICE 1: Friends, have you tried HEP HEP Magic Scouring Pads? They are useful for every member of the family.

VOICES: *(singing)*

I'm the happy pad mom uses
For the washing. What she chooses
Is always Hep Hep scouring pads.

I'm the happy pad for daddy,
I make Dad a happy laddy,
He says Hep Hep is the finest he has had.

I'm the gentle one for sister, I don't
Scrape or blister,
When she washes with old Hep Hep scouring pads.

When Junior comes indoors
Filled with dirt and awful odors,
You'll find Hep Hep is the best help you have had.
There is no finer pad than the Hep Hep you have had.
'Cause HEP HEP is the washing pad of stars!

VOICE 1: So radio and TV, the brain child of man,
Where genius and intellect work hand in hand
Appeal to the senses and lead us astray.
Though we rebel and resist and swear off every day
Radio and TV are here to stay!

SQUEETIES

Have you tried the new SQUEETIES? This is the breakfast food that kiddies love. They don't crunch, they don't crackle, they don't popple . . . they just lie there in the bowl and soak up milk. For a new treat, try . . . SQUEETIES.

LYE SCOUR TOOTH PASTE

We dare them all! Yes, friends, we dare them all to bring out a toothpaste that can outperform the old, time-tested LYE SCOUR toothpaste. After one use you have absolutely no problem with tooth decay. This is because of the built-in ingredient, Rootzanall. Ole Olson tried LYE SCOUR on his teeth, one at a time; and daily you can hear him say, "There goes another vun."

UP

"Don't come any closer." Is that what your friends are saying? Do you suffer from offensive breath? Have you discovered your relatives trying to back you into a garbage pail? Then get UP. Yes, get UP today for a tantalizing breath. No longer will people drop dead when you enter the room, no longer will folks stampede when you approach the crowd. And remember . . . UP spelled backwards, is PU.

DR. TIGER'S TOOTH POWDER PRESENTS . . .

DR. TIGER'S TOOTH POWDER presents Knickerbocker Marry-go-Round, starring Marian L. Marian, Thomas K. Thomas, and John Charles John. Now we take you to all the little night spots of the lower slum district.

FIRE CIGARETTES

The makers of FIRE Cigarettes bring the world's latest news events right to your living room. Sit back, light a Fire, and see what has happened on the news front during the last twenty-four hours. Fire News Caravan presents today's news *today*. Produced for FIRE cigarettes by BVD.

FIRE

Friends, you have been asked to try everything, but have you tried FIRE?

You can't beat FIRE when you want to . . .

light a cigarette

commit arson

do away with a witch

roast a whole sheep

We have this testimonial from Casey Reed. When he first tried fire he said, "Owww!!!*?:!"

Insist on FIRE. It was good enough for Nero and it's good enough for you.

QUEEN-SIZE CIGARETTES

Does your throat itch? Do harsh King-Size cigarettes make your lungs come up for air? Do you know what you need? You need CRAZY QUEEN-SIZE Cigarettes. Crazy is longer by 2,296,464½ puffs than most King-Size Cigarettes. Crazy has the new Safilter. The Safilter is 100 per cent tobacco for your protection and pleasure. Friends, after you smoke the cigarette you can smoke the filter, thus doubling the economy. And remember, Crazy Cigarettes do not contain *less nicotine!* The manufacturers have added 40 per cent more nicotine, giving you more nicotine for your money. A young man in his nicotines said, "I'm nuts about Crazy Queen-Size Nicotinized Cigarettes!" CRAZY QUEEN-SIZE Cigarettes are developed, produced, concocted, manufactured, sold, bought, and consumed by the kiddies at Kindly Old Mother Mabel's Boarding School for Disabled Dope Addicts under five.

PERSONALITY MINUS

Friends, do you wake up in the morning, feeling great? Do you feel good all day? If so, you may be suffering from Exius Costos Fosto (which is sometimes known as happiness, energy, and good health.)

This condition can be remedied only by the use of PER-

SONALITY MINUS. This wonderful product makes you wake up feeling terrible. You feel terrible all day. Personality Minus makes you scowl at everybody. Personality Minus makes you feel good about feeling bad. Personality Minus is a secret blend of opium, nicotine, hydrofluoric acid, heroin, caffein, and alcohol. Get PERSONALITY MINUS . . . today!

CHEAT SHEET

High school students, do algebra problems get you down? Does your English teacher make you use everything but good English? Then you may need Sharpie Bill Fink's special high school CHEAT SHEET. This contains such useful information as: Why Elmira Zilch lied to Dr. Kinsey, The Science of Tiddle-de-winks, why your best friends can't get close enough to tell you, and many other useful and interesting topics. Use this special Cheat Sheet for one week and see if you don't get expelled! Send in the top of your principal's desk and $3,000 for packaging, shipping, handling to Sharpie Bill Fink, Box 1195, Hades, Texas. If you are not satisfied return the CHEAT SHEET, and Bill Fink will return your principal's desk top and send your name to the principal.

GORY COMICS

Children, be sure to stop at the Zilch Kiddie Bookshop for your newest edition of GORY COMICS. We bring you a sample story at this time called "Me! The Judge!":

"I felt the sting of the bullet entering my side just as I jumped over the desk into Big Boy's stomach. The warm blood was over me when I kicked his teeth into the rear section of his mouth. He was on his feet in a toothless condition when I laid him out with a few bursts from my pocket burp gun. I started to jab my fingers in his eyes when he said,

" 'Here come the cops. Stop!'

"I told him, 'No.'

"He asked me, 'Why?'

"I said, 'Well, boy, that's the way the old ball bounces. That's the way I go about earning my livelihood!' A smile came over my face as I slowly but surely pushed him out the window.

" 'Well, Fuzz, I see you beat me to him,' said the chief as he came through the door.

" 'No,' I said, 'he beat me to him.'

" 'How's that?'

" 'He committed suicide!' "

Parents, come down and personally select some of these fine, thrilling stories for your children. There is nothing like good literature to stop the present juvenile delinquency wave. Visit Kiddies' Bookshop today.

SELF-DUNKING DOUGHNUT

Friends and neighbors, have you tried Daddy Parkington's new product, DUNK-SELF, the amazing, all-new, self-dunking doughnut?

Dunk-Self is the doughnut that has an affinity for coffee. It jumps off the plate right into the cup, and jumps right out of the cup back onto the plate, ready to eat. Dunk-Self saves you the trouble of getting your hands into the coffee. Why not pick up a bag of DUNK-SELF—today?

NOTHING

Have you tried NOTHING?

William Shakespeare first made it famous when he wrote the play, "Much Ado About . . . " And as Ben Grogan says of his golf, "Nothing is better than a hole in one." Homer Valentine says, "Nothing is better than lying in the sun and fishing all day." Many of your friends prefer NOTHING. Next time try it yourself.

THE STORY OF SHIRLEY AND JIM

ANNOUNCER:

We take great pleasure in presenting the story of Shirley and Jim, average teen-age boy and girl. For those who have missed the last thrilling chapter, here is a brief résumé of what has happened:

Mr. Krantz, the principal of Gainesburg High School and the head of the local Fascist party, had just told Bee that Irma could not be trusted because she had testified before the City Council that she knew several people in the Fascist party. She said that she had learned this from Susie's boy friend, Val, who in turn had learned it from Courtney's valet, Harvey, who was, at one time, a member. As he arrived at the weekly meeting, Max's brother, Sidney, saw Margie's son, Bruce, kissing Shan's daughter, Phyllis. He was just about to say something when Mr. Krantz called the meeting to order. As soon as the meeting was over, Sidney went straight to Attorney Benson's house to tell him of the strange relationship between Edgar and Alice . . . the same Alice who came to Cynthia's party three hours late only to find that the party was over. But, as Joan's English teacher, Miss Hargrave, expressed it to Frank's girl friend, Flo, it was just a matter of time! And now our story starts with Jack and Emily, Temple and Sue, Chuck and Margaret on the front lawn of the school where Jack is just about to throw a bottle of nitroglycerin onto the front porch. We hear Temple speaking.

TEMPLE: Well, hurry up!

ANNOUNCER: I'm sorry . . . I see our time is up. Tune in again for another exciting chapter in the lives of Shirley and Jim, average teen-age boy and girl!

CARBO

Friends, are you tired of drinking insipid beverages? Then turn to the new CARBO, which is pure carbonated water, with color added. Carbo gives you energy you never had before. Carbo makes you bubble all over. Carbo puts that sparkle in your voice. If you have never effervesced before, get a load of CARBO and your friends will marvel at you.

NAG-NAY

Do you suffer from nagging headaches or backaches? Does your wife or mother-in-law bother you? Are people nagging at you all the time? If so, you must try the new NAG-NAY. Nag-Nay rids you of these, plus annoying pains and disorders like tooth decay, radiation sickness, or the urge to commit suicide. Just take a Nag-Nay bath and wash your troubles away. Caution—use only as directed, for NAG-NAY will eat the tub if you use too much.

chapter 5

FILL THE GAP WITH

LONGER

STUNTS

FILL THE GAP WITH LONGER STUNTS

THE STUNTS in this chapter call for more preparation than those previously presented. All are nonsensical, and we believe they will provide good entertainment.

If you are interested in additional material of this type, see Chapter 6 in *The Handbook of Skits and Stunts* and also the catalogs of play publishers, which list many longer dramatic sketches, as well as one-act and three-act plays.

The Lover's Errand[1]

CHARACTERS: Harold, a straightforward youth with round-about methods.

Daisy, a very simple maiden.

SCENE: *The living room at Daisy's. A sofa, or two chairs, placed down Right are the necessary properties. Daisy, wearing a gingham dress, is dusting and singing. There is a knock at the door Left, and she goes to admit Harold, an awkward country boy with a large straw hat and a coat too large for him. Daisy is very coy; Harold, very bashful.*

DAISY: Oh, hello, Harold, did you come to see me?

HAROLD: No, I mean, yes—that is, I just came over to ask you somethin'.

DAISY: O-o-oh, Harold! Come over and set down on the sofa. *(They sit.)*

HAROLD: I just got a minute. I—I got to ask you somethin'. You see, Mother—she . . .

DAISY *(sentimentally)*: Yes, Harold, I understand. I always did like your mother.

[1] From R. Bruce Tom, Columbus, Ohio.

HAROLD: That so?

DAISY *(demurely)*: Yes, that's nice, isn't it?

HAROLD *(baffled)*: W-e-e-ll, I dunno. *(Then with animation)* Say, did you see where Jim Hawkin's barn burnt down last week? Gosh, I wisht I hadn't missed that fire. Ain't often we get so much excitement around Beanville.

DAISY *(moving closer)*: Now, Harold, you didn't come over to tell me about the fire.

HAROLD *(admiringly)*: Gosh, Daisy, how'd you know that?

DAISY: A woman's understanding, I guess.

HAROLD: Sounds more like mind reading to me.

DAISY *(moving closer as Harold squeezes himself into his corner)*: Now, Harold, you ain't afraid to speak up, are you?

HAROLD: Say, guess you didn't hear me speak up in experience meetin' last week, did you? Parson said I was gettin' right good in speakin' up!

DAISY *(moving closer)*: I—I'd like to hear you speak up right now, Harold.

HAROLD *(somewhat perplexed)*: Don't seem like this here's the proper time or place, Daisy.

DAISY: W-e-e-ll, Pa's out in the barn and Ma's gone down the road a piece. There ain't no one here but you and me, Harold.

HAROLD: No, I couldn't speak up nohow. 'Taint the same. You come 'round to meetin' next week. Then I will.

Daisy plumps herself down on other end of sofa, pouts. Harold looks at her in dumb surprise.

HAROLD: Now you ain't mad at me, Daisy?

DAISY: Well, ain't you goin' to tell me what you came for, Harold?

HAROLD: W-e-e-ll, I got somethin' to ask you.

DAISY: Y-e-es?

HAROLD: Maybe I better wait and ask your Ma.

DAISY: Oh, Ma don't care.

HAROLD: Gosh, I wisht it was over with!

DAISY: A-a-aw, Harold! That ain't a nice way to talk.

HAROLD: Well, I got the milkin' to do and drive Jerusha down to the blacksmith's. Beats all the way she throws her shoes.

DAISY: Guess you don't think I've got nothing to do but set here.

HAROLD: Well, I might just as well ask you and get it over with.

DAISY (*a-flutter with expectation*): Yes, Harold, go right ahead. I'm listenin'.

HAROLD (*getting up and going toward the door*): Guess— guess some other time'll do just as well. Guess I might as well be gettin' along home.

DAISY (*going over to him*): You jest ain't got spunk enough to ask me, that's what.

HAROLD (*desperately*): Well, I'm a-goin' to ask you. . . . I'm goin' to ask you right now. Mother sez for me to ask you kin she borry your petticoat pattern!

DAISY (*furious and disappointed*): Yes, she kin have it, and don't you ever come sneakin' around in here askin' me any more questions, Harold Jenkins. I never want to see you again!

She flounces out Right.

HAROLD: Gosh, I sure feel sorry for the feller who marries *her!*   CURTAIN

The Curing Machine[2]

SCENE: *The doctor's office. A large, impressive improvised machine is there, with a special connection for a patient, and one for the dummy.*

CHARACTERS: The doctor, his nurse, her boy friend, four patients.

DOCTOR: Miss Sippi, will you come here a minute?

[2] From Russell Schaeffer, Tarentum, Pa.

NURSE: Yes, doctor?

DOCTOR: I want to show you our new machine that cures any ill.

NURSE: That's wonderful, Doctor. How do you do it?

DOCTOR: Why, you take this cap and put it on a patient, like this. *(Shows her.)* Then you transfer the illness of the patient into the dummy.

NURSE: And where is the dummy?

DOCTOR: He hasn't come in yet. We have the shipping papers on him.

NURSE: Well, that certainly is a wonderful invention if it works.

Her boy friend comes in.

NURSE: Oh, hello, Raymond, dear.

RAYMOND: Hi, Sally! Hi, doc! Just dropped in for a minute, on my way back to the store from lunch.

NURSE: Here, let us show you the machine that the doctor has. It will cure anything. You put the cap on this way *(shows him)* and the illness of the patient is transferred to the dummy right over here.

RAYMOND: Where's the dummy?

NURSE: He hasn't come in yet. We have the shipping papers.

DOCTOR: Say, I believe there's a patient coming. See if there is, Miss Brown. Quick, Raymond, let me hook you over here where the dummy is supposed to be.

RAYMOND: Oh, no! I'm all right and I want to stay that way!

DOCTOR: I'll pay you ten dollars a patient to sit over there.

RAYMOND: That's more like it. I'll take a try.

DOCTOR: Hurry, now! *(Attaches machine to Raymond.)*

PATIENT *(entering, with hand up in air):* Doctor, my hand is giving me some trouble. I have heard about your machine. Can you help me?

DOCTOR: Sure! *(Fastens cap on patient, runs machine. Suddenly patient lowers hand, Raymond raises his.)* See, you're cured.

PATIENT: Thank you so much, doctor. I'm cured! Here's twenty-five dollars.

DOCTOR: Thank you. Be sure to tell others.

NURSE: Here's another patient, doctor.

SECOND PATIENT *(jerking):* Doctor, I've got a nervous affliction. If you can cure me, I'll give you $100.

DOCTOR: Thank you, my friend. I have utmost confidence in the machine. Let us put this cap on you. *(Does so, turns on machine, patient stops jerking, Raymond starts jerking, hand up in air also.)* See, you're cured!

PATIENT: Thank you so much, doctor. Here's the money. *(Leaves.)*

NURSE: Doctor, your fame is spreading! Here's another patient.

THIRD PATIENT: Doctor, I've had an awful time. I was kicked by a mule, and ever since then I've been pawing the earth. See? *(Shows him the affliction.)* If you can cure me, I'll give you $200.

DOCTOR: You are as good as cured. Take a seat and let us fasten this cap on you. *(Does so, and patient paws the floor. Soon he stops, Raymond starts, adding to the other afflictions.)* See, you're cured.

PATIENT: Thank you, doctor. You have relieved me greatly. *(Pays and leaves.)*

NURSE: Here's a . . . gentleman . . . to see you, doctor.

BUM *(enters, scratching):* Doc, I've just heerd of your curing machine.

DOCTOR: Yes, it's a wonder. What is your trouble?

BUM: Well, I've been putting off seeing somebody. I've had this itching for three years.

RAYMOND *(who is jerking and pawing, with hand up in the air):* Oh, no! Oh, no! I don't mind these so much, but I'm not going to have the seven-year itch for love *nor* money! *Rushes off stage for curtain or blackout.*

Political Rally

Our speaker talks in the manner of the noisy political orator. He is loud, waves arms, is forceful. He will need to hold for laughs and, when he has made a point, may want to use handkerchief, get a drink of water, or whatever, to give the audience time.

SCENE: A political rally, the speaker on an improvised platform, which contains other dignitaries. There is a small "audience" in front of the speaker, and the voices and hecklers speak from there. However, they might speak from the entire audience.

Band music will add flavor, either recorded music or an improvised band (even with kitchen instruments). Also, a Master of Ceremonies could encourage the crowd to cheer.

Many of the phrases used actually came from the language of a national political convention.

CHAIRMAN *(using gavel):* Silence, please, friends. Silence! Silence!

Ladies and gentlemen, we are here to rally to the cause of our grea-a-at political party, the Repugnocrats. Yes, my friends, and the man who is to lead this grea-a-at rally is one of the finest men this county has ever produced. Yes, I say without fear of any contradiction that our speaker is a man of broa-a-ad background, a man of grea-a-at proportions. He loves people. He loves men and women and babies. Why, just the other day I saw him showing his affection to one of the prettiest babes in the county—she was just about sixteen Yes, he stands with Thomas Jefferson, George Washington, Abraham Lincoln, ———— (fill in some local name), and a-a-all the grea-a-at men in the country. Here is a self-made man. I present to you, Charles P. Blowhard.

BLOWHARD: Mr. Chairman and friends. *(He is stuffed with*

pillows to make him a man of great proportions). Yes, I say, *friends*. (Don't you say you are not my friends. Nobody's gonna tell me who my friends are.)

Today we stand at the crossroads of history. We are bewildered, frustrated, alarmed. We find that people are looking to our party to save their liberty. Yes, my friends, we stand at the crossroads of destiny, but all the more we will be assured of the victory!

Yes, friends, we have a grea-a-at party. We have learned how to work closely together. My opponents claim that we cannot keep the party together, but I want to tell you that just here in the county seat last Saturday night we had a rally and it took eleven deputy sheriffs to pull them apart!

Now, my friends, I want to say to you that I am conducting my campaign on a high plane, but my opposition is not doing the same. Just before I came over here, I am sure that they got someone to throw a *cowardly egg* at me.

VOICE: Just what is a cowardly egg, sir?

BLOWHARD: My friend, that's an egg that hits you and runs. (*Continues.*) Yes, my friends, I am encouraged about the party. I believe we are developing a spurit of unity and common interest. This dense crowd here today shows it.

HECKLER: Maybe we ain't as dense as you think.

BLOWHARD: Now, my friends, I want to say that my opponent is *not* a worthy man. He has been using deception on you, friends and neighbors. When I even consider the possibility of the election of such a man, I view the future with alarm. *This man* is a *demagogue!*

VOICE: What's a demagogue?

BLOWHARD: That, my friend, is a man who can rock the boat and then make everybody think there is a terrible storm at sea! Yes, my friends, if you don't want an extremist to serve you in this high office, you should elect me. I am an experienced middle-of-the-road man.

VOICE: Where did you get your experience?

BLOWHARD: I was a bus driver for ten years. *(Continues.)* Yes, we must think this through. We must take notice of the dangers facing our party. We must learn a lesson from history. *(Stops dramatically and holds up both hands.)* Pause, friends . . .

VOICE: Yeah, two of them *(meaning "paws")*—and dirty ones, too.

BLOWHARD: Well, to get on with my speech. I want to tell you that I believe in the principles of Aberham Lincoln, Thomas Jefferson, and a-a-all of the great leaders of the past. I believe, my friends, in that old American principle, "the greatest good for the greatest number."

LADY: What do you consider the greatest number?

BLOWHARD: Lady, I consider the greatest number . . . number *one*! Yes, as I say, we must resolve our differences in the traditional American way. We stand in a solid phalanx if we are to win!

VOICE: What does phalanx mean?

BLOWHARD: I don't rightly know, but if my opponent stands there, I do too. As I say, we must take a firm, forthright, fighting stand against the flauntings of the future. We must get rid of radicalism!

VOICE: That's right. Radicalism.

BLOWHARD: And socialism.

VOICE: Yes, socialism.

BLOWHARD: Bolshevism.

VOICE: Bolshevism.

BLOWHARD: Anarchism.

VOICE: Yes, anarchism.

BLOWHARD: Yes, my friends, I can help you get rid of any of these "isms." Is there one I have not named?

ANOTHER VOICE: Help *me*, then, Blowhard. I've got rheumatism!

MAN (*just arriving at back of crowd, speaks to another*): Who is speaking?

ANSWER: That's our friend Blowhard.

MAN: What's he talking about?

ANSWER: He hasn't said.

BLOWHARD: You want a man who has a program, a positive program. Well, I want to tell you farmers that I was bor-r-rn on a farm. I'm a practical farmer. I can mow hay with the best of 'em; I can milk with the best of 'em. In fact, friends and neighbors, I challenge this audience right now to tell me one useful thing on the farm that I cannot do! (*Pauses dramatically.*)

VOICE: Say, mister . . . can you lay an egg?

BLOWHARD: We must have prosperity, and to have prosperity we must grow more corn. I believe in price subsidy for corn. We must grow more wheat. I believe in price support for wheat. We must grow more beans. I believe in subsidy for beans.

VOICE: Well, what about *hay*?

BLOWHARD: Right now I'm talking about human food. We'll come to yours in a minute. Now, let us turn to the wool crop. As an old-time farmer, friends, I must ask you to take care about our wool. If we don't stop shearing the wool off the sheep that lays the golden egg, we'll soon find we have pumped it dry!

Yes, my friends, if elected I will get jobs for all of you. I propose to build a grea-a-at bridge across the Mississippi River, the great Mississippi on whose banks you stand. There will be millions of jobs.

VOICE: But it won't take millions of people to build a bridge across the river.

BLOWHARD: Yes, it will—the way I'm gonna do it. Friends, I propose to build this great bridge across the river—lengthwise!

Now in closing I want to say a few last words. I want

land reform. I want housing reform. I want prison reform, I want *(stops for climax)* . . .

VOICE *(good and loud):* Chloroform!

BLOWHARD: Good bye, my friends. Your vote and influence
appreciated.

Band plays as he leaves.

We Introduce, with Pride[3]

Friends, fellow citizens, and others . . . I feel that we
would pass by a great opportunity if we failed to pay tribute
on this momentous occasion to the young gentleman who
has in so large a measure been responsible for what we
enjoy here today.

He has been prominent in political circles for many cam-
paigns. He has spread his fame to the four corners of the
country. It is my honored privilege to present for our ap-
proval this sterling young gentleman, this silver-tongued orator, this man of the hour—Joe Doaks [or a local person]!

Joe Doaks was born in [nearby town], at the age of six.

Joe Doaks was born in ———, ———, but don't hold
that against him. He couldn't help that.

At an early and tender age, he moved to ———, ———,
and ——— County, where at the age of ten he was the best-
known child in the neighborhood. At the age of fifteen he
was the most quoted boy in town. At the age of eighteen
he was the favorite son of the township. At the age of twenty-one, he was known the length and breadth of the entire
county.

He was elected county judge with a salary of $3,500 a
year. So well did he adapt himself to the duties and oppor-
tunities of that office that at the end of his term, he had
saved up one hundred thousand dollars. And bear in mind,
my friends, he was born a *poor boy.*

In the last election, my friends, Joe Doaks received in his

[3] From Howard Ellis, Nashville, Tenn.

own precinct not one single vote, and he knows definitely, he knows positively, that there was a needle in that haystack. His mother might have double-crossed him. Even his wife might have double-crossed him. But he knows doggoned well he voted for himself.

They have accused us of slinging mud in this campaign, my friends. And we admit it. But if we have been slinging mud, what have they been slinging? Not what you think. They have been slinging eggs! And, oh, what eggs!

They have told you that while making a speech in ———, ———, Joe Doaks was struck with a dead cat. It's a lie. A dirty, bare-face lie. It was not in ———. It was in ———. And not only that, it was not a dead cat. It was a skunk! And believe me, it was far from dead.

Joe Doaks has served the people of this state with rare distinction for many years. He served as county dogcatcher through two terms. If time permitted, we could tell you of the effect and esteem in which he is held by the stray dogs of this community. Both Falla and Checkers have paid tribute to the efficient way in which he has discharged the duties that have attended this office.

We can only promise you that if Joe Doaks is elected, the people will get exactly what is coming to them.

In closing, my friends, we can only say for Joe Doaks, as he has said again and again, and I quote in the words of that honored American: "All that I am, all that I hope to be, I owe to that honored example of American life and thought, Horatio Alger!"

NOTE: *If there is no one in the group that is being especially "honored" by this campaign speech, the toastmaster may, of course, make his speech for himself in the first person for added effectiveness. In which case the punch line may be at the close, with the presentation of the name of the candidate, in typical campaign fashion.*

Up from the Doorstep[4]
Or, The Orphan Girl's Triumph

CHARACTERS

Flagstone Grimm, Superintendent of the Little Sunshine Asylum for Female Orphans
Comly Grimm, his son
Lillyella, the Orphan Asylum drudge
Fred Saltonstall, the milkman
Six little Orphan Girls

SCENE: *Dining room of the orphanage, early evening. Six children are at the table; one is crying.*

FIRST ORPHAN: Please, please stop crying.

SECOND ORPHAN: My tummy hurts. Boo-oo-hoo!

THIRD ORPHAN: She's hungry. Mr. Grimm made her go without breakfast and dinner.

FOURTH ORPHAN: Because she asked for more hash last night.

FIFTH ORPHAN: I'm hungry, too, and I didn't miss any meals.

SIXTH ORPHAN: Me, too, I'm hungry!

ALL: We're hungry. Our stummicks hurt too! *(They set up a howl. Lillyella enters, Left. She wears a wig with long golden curls, and is dressed in faded tatters. Her voice is always sugar-sweet, and her manner coy. She carries a large tray with six bowls on it.)*

LILLYELLA *(looking around in dismay):* Why, children dear, whatever is the matter?

ALL: We're hungry!

LILLYELLA: Of course you are. But just wait until you see what we have for supper.

ALL *(eagerly):* What? What?

LILLYELLA *(starting to set a bowl at each place):* Rice pudding!

[4] By Sara Bulette. Reprinted by permission of the Countrywomen's League, Curtis Publishing Co., Philadelphia 5, Pa.

FIRST ORPHAN: We can't eat that yet.

LILLYELLA *(taken aback):* Why?

FIRST ORPHAN: Rice pudding is for dessert. How can you eat dessert without something else first? *(She begins to cry, and the others follow suit.)*

LILLYELLA *(aside to audience):* Oh, dear! Oh, dear! What shall I do? *(Suddenly she stops wringing her hands and turns smiling to children.)* Hush, darlings! Put your dessert to one side and I'll bring in the other courses. How silly of me to forget! *(Exit, Left, and re-enters almost immediately, carrying an empty tray as though it were loaded with dishes. Pretends to set something at each place.)* This, dears, is your tomato juice cocktail.

THE ORPHANS: Where?

LILLYELLA: Why, I just put it in front of you.

FIRST ORPHAN: I don't see anything!

SECOND ORPHAN: What does it look like?

LILLYELLA: Each tomato juice cocktail is in a tiny glass. You drink it like milk, only it's bright red with millions of vitamins. The vitamins are so small you can't see them, but they are full of vim, vigor, and vitality.

FIRST ORPHAN *(turning to child next to her):* Mine's redder'n yours!

SECOND ORPHAN: It is not! Mine's redder. And it's got more vitama-jiggers.

LILLYELLA: Now, now, darlings! They are all very red and very de-li-shuss. Pick up your glasses and sip your tomato juice daintily, like this. *(She demonstrates with imaginary glass, holding her little finger straight out in the air. The children do likewise, beginning to enjoy themselves immensely. Lillyella pretends to clear table, goes out and returns with tray.)* And here's the main course—all dressed up for our party. Lamb chops with white paper frills, potatoes baked in little brown jackets. And buttered carrots to make your hair curly!

THE ORPHANS: Hurrah for Lillyella! *(They watch eagerly, while Lillyella pretends to set dishes in front of them, and faithfully go through gestures of cutting and eating, prompted by Lillyella.)*

FIRST ORPHAN *(as Lillyella pretends to clear table):* My hair isn't getting curly yet!

SECOND ORPHAN: It will, though, any minute. I bet we ate a whole peck of carrots. *(Looking tearful)* B-but I'm still hungry!

LILLYELLA *(quickly):* Now you can eat your DESSERT. And look at it, my dears. Don't you see something unusual about this rice pudding?

FIRST ORPHAN: It's real.

SECOND ORPHAN: It's white and thick.

LILLYELLA *(triumphantly):* That's because it has honest-to-goodness milk in it!

THIRD ORPHAN *(accusingly):* You know Mr. Grimm doesn't allow you to use milk to make rice pudding.

LILLYELLA: This milk was a present—to me *(coyly casting down eyes)* from Fred the milkman. He said he wanted to present me with a token of his esteem. I told him I could not possibly accept a present from a gentleman—but a bottle of milk would be different.

ALL: Good for Lillyella! Let's eat. *(They pick up their spoons and are about to attack the pudding when Mr. Grimm enters, Right Center, scowling.)*

MR. GRIMM: What is the cause of this unseemly commotion?

LILLYELLA *(shrinking):* Nothing, sir. Oh, nothing, I assure you!

MR. G: Speak when you are spoken to! *(Turns to children.)* We shall have no idle chatter at the table. *(All sit with hands in laps, eyes downcast. Mr. Grimm notices pudding. He picks up a spoon and dips into First Orphan's bowl.)* Rice pudding! *(Starts.)* WITH MILK IN IT! And a raisin! *(He gulps spoonful.)*

LILLYELLA *(anxiously):* Indeed, sir, there were no raisins!

FIRST ORPHAN: A fly fell in. He drowned. *(The others snicker, as Mr. Grimm sputters.)*

MR. G. *(recovering):* Leave the table at once—every last one of you! *(Children shrink past him to Exit, Right Center, looking longingly back at untouched rice pudding. Lilly-ella starts to follow. Mr. G. grabs her roughly by the wrist.)* Stay, wench! I am not through with you.

LILLYELLA *(humbly):* I am very sorry, sir, about the fly, sir.

MR. G.: I have not heard you deny there was MILK in the rice pudding. Who is responsible for this gross extravagance?

LILLYELLA *(with head high):* I, and I alone, am responsible. *(Hastily, with less assurance.)* But it did not cost the Little Sunshine Asylum for Female Orphans anything, sir.

MR. G. *(impatiently):* Pray do not speak in riddles!

LILLYELLA: The milk was a present *(striking a pose of maidenly modesty)* to me.

MR. G.: And who would give *you* a present?

LILLYELLA *(with dignity):* A gentleman, sir, by the name of Mr. Fred Saltonstall.

MR. G.: Who is this *gentleman*?

LILLYELLA: Mr. Saltonstall delivers milk to the family in the adjoining premises. *(Mr. G. is about to explode with wrath when Lillyella continues hastily.)* When I scrub the front steps at daybreak he always bids me good day as he goes by—in the most gentlemanly manner imaginable, sir. We have never been formally introduced, but I feel that I know him. And when he offered to buy me a present I said I would rather have a bottle of milk, sir, if he could spare one.

MR. G.: Accepting presents from strange milkmen! This is an outrage. *(He raises his arm, flourishing arm in air. Lilly-ella cringes away from him.)* To think I have sheltered this scourge—this blot on the fair name of womanhood—within the walls of this noble institution among innocent mortals of tender and impressionable disposition! *(He lowers arm, then dramatically points to doorway.)* Leave at once and never darken this door again!

LILLYELLA *(who has fallen to her knees with arms outstretched):* Oh, please, sir, do not turn me from the only shelter I have known since I was left on your doorstep sixteen long years ago with a silver spoon in my mouth *(aside to audience, with a deep sigh)* or so they say. I have never seen the spoon.

MR. G. *(aside to audience):* She is a comely wench. Perhaps . . . *(leers wickedly).*

LILLYELLA: Ah, sir, if you would reconsider!

MR. G. *(still aside to audience while Lillyella kneels with face buried in her hands):* After all, she is the only one who can handle those boisterous orphan brats. And now, as never before, they must be kept out from underfoot. *(Places hand over heart.)* My dear son is returning from his university today. Ten long years since I have clasped him to this paternal bosom. *(Folds arms.)* He must not suspect that I have snatched the very food from the orphans' mouths to buy the stocks that soared to make our fortune. No, he must never suspect, for he admires me as a great philanthropist.

LILLYELLA *(looking up entreatingly):* Have pity on a hapless orphan girl!

MR. G.: You are a disgrace to the Little Sunshine Asylum for Female Orphans. *(Aside to audience)* Only this wench can help me keep the truth from my adored son.

LILLYELLA *(throwing her arms about his knees):* Sir! Sir! Does there flash across that countenance a glimmering of mercy? Ah, relent! Relent!

MR. G. *(pushing her roughly away):* Get to your feet, miserable female! *(Lillyella, trembling, rises.)* The warm humanity of my nature bids me give you one more chance.

LILLYELLA *(clasping her hands):* Henceforward I shall work my fingers to the bone to prove how strong the gratitude of one weak woman can be.

MR. G.: Enough of empty verbiage. Go now to the children. Keep them out of the way for the rest of the evening. My son returns tonight from a great eastern university. We shall not wish to be disturbed.

LILLYELLA: I hasten to obey. *(Runs mincingly toward doorway, Right Center, pauses and turns as she reaches it.)* I fear I have at times misjudged you. *(Clasps hands at bosom, gazing heavenward.)* But now I know that stern visage and haughty mien are but the bulwarks of a noble and sensitive nature. *(Coyly)* You are indeed a man any girl could look up to. *(Exit, Right Center. Mr. Grimm, looking mightily pleased with himself, struts to motto hanging on wall above sofa and straightens it, then stands with hands behind back, lost in pleasant thought. Comly Grimm appears in doorway, Right Center, hat in one hand, suitcase in the other. He gazes contemptuously at his father.)*

COMLY *(to audience):* To think that that softhearted jellyfish should be *my* father! No doubt at this very moment he is concocting some extravagance to lavish on his miserable waifs. And waiting for me to help him carry on his noble and self-sacrificing work. Ha! Ha! Little does he reckon I scheme to filch what funds are left and fly. But soft, I must gain his confidence. *(Placing suitcase on floor and hat on top of suitcase, he takes a long step toward his father, arms outstretched.)* Father! *(Mr. G. turns quickly, and they embrace.)*

MR. G.: Ah, my son! I have waited an eternity for this proud moment.

COMLY: And I, Father, felt I could no longer postpone the day when I took my place at your side.

MR. G.: Your place is ready, and it is no humble one. I have not been idle in these years while you were acquiring the poise and polish of the world. I have scrimped and saved the miserable stipend I allow myself as compensation for conducting this noble institution and invested it all in certain gilt-edged stocks.

COMLY *(aside):* The pickings are richer than I had bargained for. *(To his father with a flourish)* Together we shall dedicate it to the service of humanity. But let us discuss these matters tomorrow. You seem overweary from the devoted labor of a long day. As for me—my journey has been a tedious one. I am sorely in need of rest.

MR. G.: Forgive me! All such considerations were forgotten in a father's selfish joy. Wait but a moment while I see that a room is prepared for you. *(Exit Left. Comly saunters toward cupboard, Left. Lillyella enters, Right Center. She does not notice Comly, but advances to table and starts to stack bowls.)*

COMLY *(aside):* What beautiful creature is this? Never have I beheld a face so fair, a form so divine! *(Deep sigh)* She shall be mine! *(He walks quickly to Lillyella and takes a bowl from her hands.)* Such menial work desecrates your queenly fingers.

LILLYELLA *(all a-flutter):* Oh, sir! How you startled me! *(Hangs head.)* And you have mistaken my identity. I am only Lillyella, the maid of all work and a hapless orphan.

COMLY *(aside to audience):* An easy victim of my worldly charm. *(Places his hand under Lillyella's chin and forces her to look up.)* I, Comly Grimm, shall make you a queen. Soon I shall be able to spread the riches of the great world at your dainty feet.

LILLYELLA *(blushingly):* Your promises, sir, are so glittering they lead me to wonder whether your intentions are . . . quite honorable.

COMLY: Spoken with true maidenly modesty! I can do no less than match it with manly frankness. *(Impressively)* From the moment I beheld you I hoped we might wed.

What do you say to that?

LILLYELLA *(tottering daintily sidewise, hands fluttering to bosom):* This is so sudden! I scarcely know you.

COMLY *(advancing toward her):* One little word!

LILLYELLA *(retreating across stage):* You shall have it to-morrow. *(Exit, Right, almost running.)*

COMLY *(to audience):* I must lay hands on those stocks at once—even if I have to spend the rest of the night tearing this dismal edifice apart. But soft! Here comes my father. I cannot trifle longer. He must be removed from my path at any costs. *(He moves to doorway, Right Center, pulls revolver from pocket, and stands waiting, shielded by the portiere. Mr. Grimm enters, and Comly shoots him. Mr. Grimm clutches his breast, stares at his son for one long unbelieving moment, staggers to Center stage, and falls. Comly wipes pistol on handkerchief and places it in Mr. Grimm's hand.)* None will guess my dark secret. To the world he will have died by his own hand. But time is fleeting! *(He dashes toward cupboard and starts going frantically through the drawers. Lillyella appears in doorway, Right Center, with the Six Little Orphans, in long nightgowns, clutching at her skirt.)*

LILLYELLA *(not noticing Comly but speaking to audience):* I have the strangest feeling all is not well.

COMLY *(still rummaging through cupboard, suddenly comes upon stocks and flourishes them in the air):* Aha! the necessary documents! *(Lillyella at this moment spies Mr. Grimm on floor and screams. Comly rushes to aid her. The orphans start to cry and huddle in one corner.)*

LILLYELLA: What horrible deed is this?

COMLY: Do not blame my poor father for this unconsidered act of self-destruction. The burden of his duties in this Vale of Tears proved more than he could bear. His reason snapped. There is nothing *(chokes back sob)* we can do. *(Bows head.)*

LILLYELLA *(going to him):* Oh, sir, I have no words to comfort you. *(Comly is about to take her in his arms when she turns aside coyly.)* Perhaps—we two—can make a new life for ourselves—and *(indicating the huddled orphans)* for these dear innocents who need a father's care.

COMLY *(caught off guard):* WHAT? Those sniveling brats?

LILLYELLA *(drawing herself up):* They will always remain with me!

COMLY: My patience is at an end! *(He seizes Lillyella roughly by her wrist.)* You are coming with me now—alone! *(Flourishing documents)* These purloined documents will buy us half the world! *(Drags Lillyella toward doorway. Orphans set up a louder howl.)*

LILLYELLA: No! NO! *(Half fainting)* Oh, who will save a frail, defenseless female from a fate worse than death?
Fred Saltonstall appears in doorway, Right Center, wearing overalls and brandishing a bottle of milk.

FRED: I, Fred Saltonstall, will save you! *(Advances to Comly with milk bottle poised ready for action.)* Unhand that woman!

COMLY *(letting go of Lillyella and cringing):* Curses! I am undone.

LILLYELLA *(running to Fred):* This man *(pointing to Comly)* is not to be trusted! He has not recited all his dastardly deeds, but I fear those document in his hands were stolen —over the dead body of his father. *(Points to Mr. Grimm. Fred snatches the documents from Comly, goes over them quickly, and tosses them carelessly on the floor. Comly scrambles on his knees to retrieve them.)* Will you leave him his ill-gotten gains?

FRED: A thousand shares of Consolidated Tin Foil. Not worth the rubber band around them. *(Comly sinks to the floor with a groan, the documents falling from his hands. MR. GRIMM'S CORPSE SUDDENLY SITS UP.)*

MR. GRIMM: *What?* *(Lillyella screams.)* What did you say?

FRED (*patronizingly*): Completely worthless, the whole lot!
(*Mr. Grimm falls back on floor again. Orphans run to Fred
and Lillyella.*)

LILLYELLA: This is no place for these poor innocents.

FRED: Come, my dears, my trusty wagon is at the door, with
a bottle of milk for each and every one. Let us fare forth
together from this dark and evil place into the sunshine of
the wide, wide world.

LILLYELLA: You make the great world sound like such a
friendly place. I shall not be afraid to face it with your
strong right arm around me.

*Fred puts his arm around Lillyella, and they lead the chil-
dren out through the doorway, Right Center, as curtain
closes.*

Beauty and the Clock[5]

(For an all-woman audience)

SCENE: *A yard.*

PROPS: *Bench, magazines, chalk for marking clock, large
circle for clock face.*

CHARACTERS

    Alice, who is on the chubby side
    Bernice
    Cora
    Dorothy
    Evelyn, a gusher
    Freda
    Grace, who has large hips
    Hazel, showy with heavy make-up
    *Alice is seen sitting on bench on lawn with magazines open
around her. Looks glum.*

BERNICE: Hi there, Alice. What are you looking so glum
about?

ALICE: Hi, Bernice. I've got plenty to be glum about.

[5] From Tillie Bruce, Goshen, Ind.

BERNICE: What now?

ALICE: Well, I'm on the achievement day programs, and I've been thinking about what to wear.

BERNICE: Wear your blue suit. It looks lovely.

ALICE *(wailing):* I can't. It's too tight!

BERNICE: Well, Alice, it is true that you have put on some weight. Twenty-five pounds on a cow is all right . . . but on a hen, honey, it's too much.

ALICE: That's right. Well, it's coming off. I'm going on a diet.

BERNICE: Diet? That won't help. What you need is exercise, like what I take. Now, if you'd bend over and touch the floor with your finger tips without bending your knees, for ten minutes four times a day, you'd lose that awful bulge around your waist. You try it, Alice. I must run along and get my groceries. *(Hurries off stage.)*

ALICE *(feels for bulge):* Bulge? Hmmmm! *(Cora comes by.)* Hi, Cora. How are you?

CORA: OK, I guess. And you?

ALICE: Not so hot. Been thinking of going on a diet, but maybe what I need is exercise.

CORA: You sure do. I noticed how fat your arms are getting. You ought to do something about them. If you'd take arm exercises twenty minutes, three times a day, I am sure it would help. You try it now, Alice. *(Rushes off stage.)*

ALICE *(feels her arms. Runs hands over stomach and hips, and sighs. Picks up magazine):* I wonder if there'd be any exercises in this?

DOROTHY *comes by:* What you looking for, Alice, recipes?

ALICE: Nope. Exercises.

DOROTHY: Exercises? You mean you're finally going to do something about that weight you put on? You know what happened last week? I came by and you were not here, but your husband was. I asked him, "Where's Alice?" and I guess he thought I said, "How's Alice," because he said, "She's round behind." So even he notices how fat you are getting. Well—my advice is to take exercises. A half-hour twice a day would reduce that round behind. Stay with it, Alice. *(She leaves.)*

Alice feels hips and sighs.

EVELYN *(gushing):* Hello, dear. One of your best friends was telling me you were going on a diet. Now, I don't want to tell you what to do, Alice, but I would like to suggest that you try exercises for those thick ankles and puffy feet and for that awful posture. It makes you look even stupider than you are . . . I mean . . . I mean . . . well, I don't mean you are that stupid, you just look stupid . . . I mean . . . I mean . . . well, so long.

EVELYN *rushes off stage.*

Alice looks at feet and ankles, and sighs. FREDA *comes by.*

FREDA: Resting a while? My, you look like you need exercise instead of that, Alice. Aren't you getting fat? I never noticed your double chin before. You should spend an hour or so a day with mud packs on your chin. If you want a neck and chin like mine, I'll be glad to tell you what I do. 'Bye now. *(She hurries off.)*

ALICE *(shakes fist after Freda):* Look like her! Huh! If anybody else tells me I'm getting fat there'll be war. Double chin! Huh! *(Hesitates.)* Well, maybe I'd better do something about my looks! *(Picks up magazine, looks through to a certain page.)* There's the beauty page. *(Reading)*

"First you make a chart like the face of a clock." Maybe I can use the big one the kids were playing with last night. *(Hunts it, pins it on post, gets chalk.)* Now, let's see. If I want to look my very best, I'd better do everything the magazine says. I'll start with my feet.

"1. Set aside one-and-a-half hours to soak feet in vinegar water." I could do that before I go to bed. *(Marks clock face from 9:00 to 10:30.)*

"2. Massage feet forty minutes each morning." *(Adds forty minutes.)*

"3. Exercise ankles, thirty minutes." *(Adds thirty minutes.)*

"4. Rub muscles in back of legs, thirty minutes." *(Add thirty minutes.)*

"5. Peddle like a bicycle fifteen minutes." *(Adds fifteen minutes.)*

"6. Flex knees twenty times, about three minutes." *(Adds three minutes.)*

GRACE *(walks by, says):* Hi, Alice. Can't stop. I'm going out to buy a girdle. You know—a device to keep an unfortunate situation from spreading. *(Motions with her hands as she leaves.)*

ALICE *(Picks up where she left off):*

"7. Now the exercise for thighs, thirty minutes." *(Marks off thirty minutes.)*

"8. Hips, thirty minutes." *(Marks off thirty more minutes.)*

"9. Waist—thirty minutes." *(Looks at clock.)* Dinner time and breakfast dishes not washed. Oh, well . . .

"10. Chest. Breathe before open window five minutes."

"11. Neck and throat, thirty minutes." *(Marks thirty minutes.)*

"12. Hair massage twenty minutes night and morning."

HAZEL *(comes on stage):* What on earth are you doing, Alice?

ALICE *(showing magazines and clockface):* Scheduling the exercises I'm going to take to make me beautiful.

HAZEL *(with amazement):* You think that's all it takes to make you beautiful? It takes paint and powder and lotion and lipstick and things for your eyes and hair. It's darned expensive to be beautiful. It costs *dollars* to look like I do. *(Swings hips, goes off stage, head high.)*

ALICE *(to herself):* Oh, look at the money that woman has wasted. She can stay longer in five minutes than anyone else in a whole afternoon. *(Turns page, starts reading.)* "To have a good complexion" (that's what I need) "you" . . . now, let's see . . .

"1. Pat on Angel Kiss mud pack and leave on one hour."
(That would scare little Butchy to death.)

"2. Dash cold water over face ten minutes."

"3. Rub Brackett's Hair Conditioner on scalp one half
hour."

"4. Brush hair 100 strokes."

"5. Soak hands in Silky Soft hand lotion while napping or
about two hours." Me, with four kids and a hungry husband. Napping two hours. Whoever heard of me napping
five minutes! *(Tosses magazine away, sinks into chair.)* I
give up! I'll just have to stay as I am!

Hasty Harry[6] (By R. M. Elliot)

CAST OF CHARACTERS

Harry Brice, the hero	Movie Director
Ruth Hadley, the heroine	Cameraman
Patrick, Ruth's brother	Property and Stage Hands
Irish Cop	(not necessary)
Nurse	Narrator

PROPERTIES

An imitation movie camera made from a small wooden or
paper carton, with an empty baking powder can attached to
the front of the box to represent the camera lens, and a few
miscellaneous gadgets all mounted on a tripod or placed on
the top of a stepladder; a dagger; two shining quarters; a
policeman's badge, and club.

The entire action of the play takes place on a set arranged
to represent a movie studio. As the text is read by the narrator, who stands at one side of the stage, the actors interpret
the action in pantomime. The story should be read slowly
and dramatically. The reader should stand at a point where
he can see the players and allow them sufficient time to pantomime the action with much exaggeration but in a serious

[6] From Ford Lippold, Oswego, Ill.

vein. Costumes and lighting effects add to the effectiveness
of this stunt. Table and floor lamps can easily be converted
into needed spot and floodlights.

NARRATOR

Young Harry Brice strolled up the street (1) looking for his
  sweetheart,
When all at once he saw a sight that made him gasp and
  start, (2)
For coming toward him from the west, within his eyesight's
  range, sir,
He saw Ruth Hadley, whom he loved, conversing with a
  stranger.
His mien grew tense, his eyes flashed fire, he breathed in
  quick, short pants,
He smote his bosom, for he thought that he had lost his
  chance. (3)
And ever as he stewed, the pair, still walking side by side,
Drew nearer, stopped, and Harry swore that he'd do homi-
  cide. (4)
Then from his pocket, Harry pulled a weapon, long and keen.
Said he, "How dare you steal my girl, you roughneck, you
  spalpeen?" (5)
The stranger drew himself up straight and said, "Pray don't
  be rash!"
But Harry crouched and circled round, just itching for the
  clash. (6)
Then sweet Ruth Hadley (7) stepped between and lectured
  Harry roundly.
"Hold on!", she called, "Know what you're at, before you
  start so grandly."
But Harry raged the worser, he raised the cruel knife, (8)
And cried, "False maiden, stand aside, I'll have this villain's
  life!" (9)
But as he raised his gleaming tool, there wandered into sight

An Irish cop with cap and club, and badge, star-shaped and bright.

Up spake the guardian of the law, "Hold'r, Newt!" he cried,

And Harry answered, "Just in time, this villain almost died."

"And wherefore," quoth the cop, "in sooth, what seems to be the matter?

Get off the sidewalk with your brawl, and cut out all this chatter."

Then Harry and the stranger, both, jumped on the fearless cop,

They mauled him and they rolled him, until he hollered, "Stop."

Then to his feet he clambered, and as he shook in fright,

The stranger used his "number ten," and put the cop to flight.

And as he ran, the rivals upon each other flew,

While sweet Ruth Hadley cringed in fright, not knowing what to do. (10)

At last young Harry weakened, the stranger whacked him well,

Till with a mighty groaning, flat to the earth he fell. (11)

Ruth Hadley shrieked in terror, (12) expecting death, or worse.

In answer came one dressed in white, a lovely, sweet, dear nurse.

She wiped young Harry's temples, and whispered, "Give him air!"

Then Ruth knelt down and held his hand, and stroked his raven hair. (13)

The stranger stood aloof and smiled, then Harry Brice came to.

He scrambled to his feet and faced his foe, as heroes do.

Then sweet Ruth Hadley spoke at last, "Deary, meet my brother Pat."

The men shook hands and Harry cried, "Well, I never thought of that."

The four then left the battlefield, the lovers, Pat and nurse,

Thought Pat, "My luck is not so bad, this nurse, she might
    look worse." (14)

Then from his hiding came the cop, he paused to view the
    scene;

He stopped and from the street, he gleaned two quarters,
    bright and clean. (15)

Now, when you see some movie shows, whether farces or
    romantics (16)

You'll know just how they have been made, if you've watched
    us in our antics.

So on behalf of Brice and Pat and the other actoreens,

I thank you for your patience, while we pulled these foolish
    scenes.

FINIS

DIRECTIONS

(1) Harry enters left. Ruth and Pat enter, from the right,
    Ruth talking.

(2) Harry stops, gasps.

(3) Harry clutches fist, strikes breast, etc.

(4) Director shakes head violently, stops everybody; shows
    Harry how to act angry. Scene repeated from beginning.

(5) Harry approaches a stranger, frames words with lips. All
    speeches given the same way.

(6) Action suited to words.

(7) Director stops everything, shows Ruth how to look
    "sweet." Much exaggeration.

(8) Very dramatically.

(9) Enter cop.

(10) Action to this point follows words.

(11) Director holds everything while he teaches Harry how
    to fall effectively; demonstrates and makes Harry do it
    several times.

(12) Nurse enters.

(13) Director poses group in different attitudes arranging po-

sitions of heads, etc. Scene is then repeated beginning with fight.

(14) Director has actors repeat departure, men look at girls with lovesick expression, girls look coy.

(15) Reader pauses while director leaves.

(16) Reader faces audience to end.

A rehearsal of this pantomime will help in acquainting each player with his or her part and the actions that are to accompany it.

chapter 6

SOME

LIKE 'EM WITH

MUSIC

SOME LIKE 'EM WITH MUSIC

Operatic Advertisements

The introduction might be that we are all accustomed to having radio and television ads come in a certain form, and we are familiar with the way advertising is run in the newspapers, but that here is the way advertising might be done at the Metropolitan Opera House.

Then some commercials could be presented, perhaps taken directly from radio, TV, magazines or newspapers, but sung in operatic style. The key to success here would be a very able person at the piano who could improvise, as well as a singer who knew enough about operatic frills and trills to make the rendition sound reasonably good.

Report to the Board

A very good pianist, clever at improvising, can take a report, place it on the piano, and by improvising and singing the words of the report, put his audience in stitches.

If such a person is available in your organization, he may help to relieve the potential later tensions by getting the group into a good frame of mind with this tomfoolery.

Organ Grinder Man

During a stunt night or program, an organ grinder man comes in, complete with monkey and tin cup, and amuses the guests. The music box is one of those that can be bought for about a dollar at toy counters, or it may be more elaborate (or even fake). The "monkey" on a string is important. He is called upon to do some tricks. Of course he will approach various guests for contributions, biting some of the coins to see if they are good. (Some novelty stores sell rubber "monkey heads.")

The "Organ Grinder" takes requests for tunes . . . then plays the same tune over and over. His "earnings" go for some good purpose in the club or organization.

Got the Grip[1]

Three men come out to sing, one carrying a traveling bag or "grip." They may be presented as the "Sewing Machine Trio."

THIRD MAN: All right, boys, let's tune up. We've got to sing good tonight for these folks.

FIRST MAN (*puts the bag down*): I wish I could, but I can't sing, Jim.

THIRD: Why's that?

FIRST: Why, I've just had the grip!

THIRD: Well, maybe Joe and I can sing, then. We'll make it a duet.

SECOND (*who has just stepped over the bag*): Jim, I can't sing either.

THIRD: Why's that?

SECOND: I've just got over the grip!

THIRD: That's too bad. (*Sees bag.*) What's this bag doing here? (*Picks it up.*)

FIRST: Now, you can't sing.

THIRD: Why?

FIRST: You've got the grip! (*Third man looks surprised, then nods solemnly, and they all leave.*)

If they are presented as the "Sewing Machine Trio," the person in charge of the program could say, "This must be the wrong group, for there was not a singer in the bunch!"

[1] From Buckeye Recreation Lab, 1950.

Sweet Music[2]

Everybody gets a lollypop, and is asked then to sing a song. (As a performance, each performer could come out so equipped.)

Bell Backs[3]

Tie bells on the backs of several performers (especially women) and have them keep time to music. This stunt also could be coupled with "Rhythmic Spelling."

The Disappearing Quartet[4]

Even though people have seen this stunt before, it is always funny to see it again with different people.

The quartet comes out, the leader smiles elaborately and bows to the woman accompanist, who begins playing. They start to sing. One of them hits a sour note. The leader stops the music, takes him outside; loud sounds of bloody murder come from out there. Then the leader comes back, and the three start singing. This is repeated until no one but the leader and accompanist are left. She hits sour notes and he takes her outside. You hear sounds, loud cries. Then this time *she* comes back, dusting off her hands.

Funiculi, Funicula[5]

Many groups have fun dividing into threes, assigning each one to sing, when asked to do it, "Ha ha ha ha" or "he he he he" or "ho ho ho ho." The leader will point unexpectedly to a group as they are singing and they are to pick up the melody at that point, but using their own syllable. To make it more active, have them stand as they sing the syllable, sit when they are through.

[2] From Tillie Bruce, Goshen, Ind.
[3] From Paul Weaver, Elgin, Ill.
[4] *Ibid.*
[5] From Mary Lib McDonald, Birmingham, Ala.

The Musical Kitchen[6]

This is a stunt for women. The ladies are working around the kitchen at a leisurely pace as the music is played in leisurely tempo. The music speeds up and they work like demons. Different moods of the music might be reflected in their actions and in the way they carry on.

To add color and length to this stunt, they might have Operatic Recipes. One of the women sings her way through, "Two cups of flour, ½ tsp. of butter" and so on in operatic style, to some operatic or popular tune.

An Orchestra Without Note

The presentation of this stunt might include such a statement as this: "You have heard of many orchestras of note. Here is one that simply cannot qualify, but the program committee wanted an orchestra, so here it is."

The members file out, take their chairs, either with real instruments or pantomiming instruments and, as the conductor conducts, play in keeping with his style, but not making any music at all. There may be solo instruments (the player stands), even long pauses. The musicians will play trills, will indicate rhythms with body motions. If really done in fancy style, the lighting with spotlights might pick up soloists at the proper time.

The World's Outstanding Sympathy Orchestra

The conductor takes the privilege of presenting the various members of the orchestra and their instruments. Then he indicates that this is what they modestly believe to be the outstanding sympathy orchestra in the world.

Whereupon, someone comes in and interrupts the conductor with a sad tale of woe. A girl has lost her boy friend, or a youth has just wrecked the family car, or some other catas-

[6] From Tillie Bruce, Goshen, Ind.

trophe has taken place—and great sympathy, weepings, and gnashings come from the orchestra.

Solo

A great build-up is given for the singer, who has studied everywhere, won gold medals, silver medals, bronze medals, brass medals, metal medals, and paper medals. She is announced thus: "Miss More will now sing, 'O Lord, Be Merciful!'"

The "soloist" then pantomimes the song completely, not singing a note. The accompanist plays elaborately and soulfully. The singer may end with her eyes modestly closed, bowing low to the audience.

The Base Quartet

This group is presented elaborately ("How fortunate we are to . . .") and then the members are introduced, one at a time.

There is————————————(Fill in his name), First Base.

There is————————————(Fill in his name), Second Base.

There is————————————(Fill in his name), Third Base.

Here is——————————. He sings at home.

They may then rush quickly to get themselves little "bases" and set up a small miniature baseball field and sing at their bases. "Take Me Out to the Ball Game," would be appropriate.

At the finish of the number, the leader of the quartet might say, "Friends, we have a confession to make. We originally got our name, as the Base Quartet, in another fashion. There were some people who called us that because of our low-down music, and they said it was base."

Whereupon the group asks the quartet to sing a low-down song.

The quartet then gets on the floor, chin in elbows, and sings some very harmonic song, "low down" style.

Turnabout Quartet

Without telling what is going to happen, of course, the quartet comes out and tunes up, then begins to sing; but the audience is in for a surprise. If the quartet is men, then women's voices (through the curtain or sheet right behind them) ring forth. If the quartet is girls or women, boys' or men's voices are heard. By practicing together, the two groups can work out some amazing effects.

Two in One

One person is singing, the second is behind the first, with arms in the position of the first, making the gestures (girl's arms for boy singer, vice versa). The arms make motions with which the singer must try to keep in tune.

The Opera[7]

CHARACTERS: Eight or ten girls in orchestra with a varied assortment of instruments. One, a conductor, stands in front and directs in a very exaggerated manner. The musicians never play their instruments but sing all the story, after the characters are introduced, while the characters come in and fit their acting to the words of the "orchestra."

STAGE PROPERTIES: A chair out front for the heroine and a chair back to one side of the "moon."

COSTUMES: Members of the "orchestra" should be dressed in proper costume. "Moon" wears long white robe and a large circular white cardboard around her head. "Curtains" should be dressed in long robes. When they rise they separate with a sort of skip or jump, keeping time with each other and falling in the same manner. The hero, heroine, vamp, and villain should be dressed to suit the parts.

The characters come out in this order, introducing themselves:

[7] From Margaret Evans. Buffalo, N. Y.

1. Orchestra (take their seats after introduction)
2. Curtains
3. Heroine
4. Hero
5. Villain
6. Vamp
7. Moon

The heroine, hero, villain, and vamp retire and reappear as the story proceeds. The tune is "The Bear Went Over the Mountain."

After other characters have been introduced, singing in same manner, the Moon rises. The "orchestra" sings, and the characters pantomime the following couplets:

1. The heroine waits for the hero
    But the hero doesn't come.
2. In walks the hero,
    And he's a very fine "he."
3. The hero woos the heroine,
    For she's a very fine "her."
4. The hero asks her to wed him,
    And the heroine agrees.
5. The hero goes for the ring
    And leaves the heroine alone.
6. In creeps the villain
    Much to the heroine's dismay.
7. The villain chases the heroine
    For he's a very bad "vill."
8. In presses the vamp
    To vamp the villain away.
9. The villain won't be vamped
    Which causes jealousy.
10. The vamp kills the heroine
    And the heroine falls down dead.

11. The villain kills the vamp,
     For he's a very bad "vill."
12. Back comes the hero
     And finds the heroine dead.
13. The hero kills the villain,
     For he must get revenge.
14. The hero dies of grief
     And falls down beside his love.

Moon sets. Curtains down. Curtains up. All characters appear and sing

ALL: We are the opera
      And we are a very good opera
      We are the opera
      And we are a very fine OPERA.

CURTAIN

Singing Scarecrows[8]

Set the stage with cornstalks or a shock and pumpkins, if this is to be in the fall. Scarecrows may be constructed with two broom handles or like-sized material, one for the body and the other placed at right angles near the top, for the arms. The crossbar arrangement may then be clothed with the oldest clothes you can find. Hay may be used for stuffing.

Make up the faces of the singers to appear colorless, with features standing out very well. Put on an old hat with hay stuck in it, and pull it down well over the eyes. Old gloves may be worn. As the curtain goes up, the singers are standing in the cornfield behind their respective scarecrow constructions, resting their chins on the top board or pole. Their arms rest on the crosspiece.

The following is a suggested parody on the song "Way Down Yonder in the Cornfield" that may be used. Doubtless you can develop others.

[8] From R. Bruce Tom, Columbus, Ohio.

WAY DOWN YONDER IN THE CORNFIELD

(Music from "Down in Mobile," *Twice 55 Green Book of Community Songs*)

Chorus: In a cornfield, in a cornfield
               We must stand here day by day
               In a cornfield.

1st Verse
SINGER: Oh, we're the boys of Scarecrowtown
ALL: Way down yonder in the cornfield
SINGERS: We can't look up, so we all look down
ALL: Way down yonder in the cornfield.

Chorus:

2nd Verse: We stand and stand and stand all day
               To frighten thievin' crows away.

3rd Verse: Gee, but the sun gets awful hot
               But no difference if school keeps or not.

4th Verse: Would somebody in the whole big nation
               Think we scarecrows need any vacation?

5th Verse: But don't you quibble or criticize
               We've formed a club and are organized.

6th Verse: We're up to date now—nothing slow
               For we've joined——————, you know.
                           (local club)

Oh, My Darling Clementine[9]

SCENE I

Forty-niner is found digging with pick and shovel. Enter Stranger. Forty-niner continues digging while they talk slowly.

STRANGER: Hi, Pard!
FORTY-NINER: Hi!

     [9] *Ibid.*

STRANGER: What 'cha doin'?
FORTY-NINER: I ain't sayin'.
STRANGER: Diggin'?
FORTY-NINER: Yeah—diggin'.
SINGERS *off stage render first verse:*

> In a cavern, in a canyon, excavating for a mine
> Dwelt a miner, forty-niner, and his daughter, Clementine.
> *(Chorus)* Oh my darling, oh my darling, oh my darling
>   Clementine,
> You are lost and gone forever, dreadful sorry, Clementine.

SCENE II

Stranger and Forty-niner on stage as before. Enter Clementine.

STRANGER *(eying Clementine in a fascinated manner as she crosses stage and exits):* Who's that likely lookin' critter?
FORTY-NINER: Who—that?
STRANGER: Yeah, that!
FORTY-NINER: That's Clementine.
STRANGER: Clementine?
FORTY-NINER: Yeah, Clementine.
SINGERS *render second verse:*

> Light was she and like a fairy, and her shoes were number
>   nine,
> Herring boxes without topses sandals were for Clementine.
> *(Chorus)*

SCENE III

(Same as Scenes I and II)

Enter ducks, followed by Clementine. (Ducks may be dramatized by five or six persons "duck walking" across stage, quacking as they go.) Stranger goes to Clementine. They walk together off stage. Clementine stumbles and falls, putting her hand in pail of water . . . giving sound effects, which may be provided by outside assistance.

CHORUS *renders third verse:*

> Drove she ducklings to the water every morning just at nine
> Hit her foot against a splinter, fell into the foaming brine.
> *(Chorus)*

SCENE IV

(Continued from Scene III)

CLEMENTINE: Blub, blub, hal-up *(pause)*. Blub, I can't swim!

STRANGER *(pause):* I cain't swim either, Clementine.

CLEMENTINE: Blub, hal-up. Guess—blub—I'll be drownin' then.

STRANGER *(sniff):* Gu-ud by, Clementine.

FORTY-NINER: Gud-by, me datter.

CLEMENTINE: Gud-blub.

SINGERS *render fourth verse:*

> Ruby lips above the water blowing bubbles soft and fine
> But alas, I was no swimmer, so I lost my Clementine.
> *(Chorus)*

SCENE V

(Continued from Scene IV)

ACTION: *Forty-niner, one duck, and the Stranger gather around Clementine's body that has been dragged from the water. After a pause and a couple of sniffles, the Forty-niner picks up a short plank and puts it at the head of Clementine, simulating a gravestone.*

SONG *(fifth verse):*

> In the churchyard in the valley, where the myrtle doth entwine
> There are rosies and other posies fertilized by Clementine.
> *(Chorus)*

SCENE VI

ACTION: *The Forty-niner and the duck leave the scene. Stranger remains. . . . Enter Clementine's baby sister . . .*

*looks at Stranger . . . looks at grave of Clementine. Baby
sister walks over to Stranger. . . . They look at each other
and walk off stage, arm in arm.*

SONG *(sixth verse):*

How I missed her, how I missed her, how I missed my
   Clementine
Till I kissed her baby sister, plum forgot my Clementine.
(Chorus)

Old King Cole

The group is divided into five sections, each of which is
given a different line to sing. When each section's turn
comes to give its line, all within that section stand and por-
tray the action, such as holding a bugle to the lips. All sections join in the two lines beginning "Happy men are we"
and in the three-line chorus; but after each section all pre-
ceding sections give their parts before returning to the
"Happy men are we" lines: *e.g.,* "Rooty toot toot, toot toot,
said the bugler" will follow right after "Mulligan again. . . ."
These single lines accumulate until, on the last verse, all parts
have been given.

ALL *sing chorus:*

Old King Cole was a merry old soul, and a merry old soul
   was he.
He called for his pipe, and he called for his bowl,
And he called for his infantry!

FIRST SECTION: "Rooty toot toot, toot toot," said the bugler.

ALL: Happy men are we. There's none so fair as can compare
   With the sound of our harmony. Hey!
   (Repeat chorus)

SECOND SECTION: "Mulligan again, by gum," said the private.

ALL: Happy men are we . . ., etc.
   (Repeat chorus)

THIRD SECTION: "Hold my horse by the head," said the captain.

ALL: Happy men are we . . . , etc.
(Repeat chorus)
FOURTH SECTION: "We want leave for a year," said the major.
ALL: Happy men are we . . ., etc.
(Repeat chorus)
FIFTH SECTION: "The army's going to the dogs," said the general.
ALL: Happy men are we . . ., etc.
(Repeat chorus, finishing with a yelled "HEY!")

Some Musical Settings[10]

These dramatizations may be produced with casts of varied sizes. They call for few rehearsals, a minimum number of lines to be memorized, and simple costumes. Best results will be had on a stage, perhaps, but a simple platform at the end of a room may be used, or they may be done "in the round."

For the greatest effectiveness, the musical part of the program should be carefully worked out.

FIRST EPISODE: OLD-FASHIONED GARDEN

The costumes are colonial. Ferns and greens, baskets of flowers, trellises, and a rustic bench and other lawn furniture help to create a lovely garden setting. A soloist in colonial dress wanders through the garden singing the first verse of the song. As she begins the chorus a group of costumed girls appear and join in the singing. A girl and boy in old-fashioned costumes appear and seat themselves on the garden bench.

SECOND EPISODE: MEMORIES

The scene opens with a little old-fashioned lady sitting in a rocker at one end of the stage or platform. A fireplace makes a very good background and can be constructed at

[10] Suggested by Mrs. L. G. Head, Jackson, Miss.

little expense with a few yards of brick paper, a little flasher or blinker plug from the dime store, amber bulbs or clear lamps, shaded by colored paper.

Dozing in the chair, the little lady dreams while a chorus or quartette whose members may take solo parts sing musical selections depicting her girlhood, school days, graduation, romance, marriage, the first child, and the faithful husband, who comes and stands by her chair.

THIRD EPISODE: DOWN BY THE OLD MILL STREAM

In front of a large pasteboard mill wheel sit an affectionate elderly couple. A chorus of ladies, in gingham dresses, aprons, and sunbonnets appear and sing "Down by the Old Mill Stream," accompanied by actions and simple dance steps.

FOURTH EPISODE: THE UMBRELLA MAN

The umbrella man enters pushing an old umbrella cart, which is a bicycle wheel surrounded by a wooden frame made from strips of lath. From its sides hang the various implements of the umbrella man's trade. Members of the chorus wear raincoats and carry colorful umbrellas and something to be mended—clocks, children's toys, and even broken hearts. A chorus sings this melody, parts of it in turn being sung by individual members of the group, with the umbrella man always adding his "toodle-i-aye."

FIFTH EPISODE: BOOTS AND SADDLE

No program would be complete without a cowboy song. From the rails of a real log fence (if at all possible) which serves as a background hang boots and saddles. Brush is burned so it can be smelled, but in a large kettle instead of under it. The branding iron is heated in an artificial fire and the imitation, behind scenes, of a bawling calf, as the branding is enacted, proves effective. Ranch costumes are worn.

Around the campfire is the usual card game, and singing to the accompaniment of a guitar as the camp cook in his sugar-sack apron stirs a pot of boiling stew. The scene ends with "Come and get it."

EPISODE SIX: SHE'LL BE COMIN' ROUND THE MOUNTAIN (first suggestion)

Stage setting—a large mountain covered with green grass blankets or painted green. The leading player appears in bright red pajamas as a soloist sings "She'll Be Coming Round The Mountain." On each succeeding stanza, two—then four, then six—white horses make their appearance. These can be made from large faces cut from cardboard and a sheet draped over two players, one stooping in front of the other. A tail of long-braided, colored paper swishes behind each horse, as he keeps in step to the music coming round the mountain. At the end the rooster's neck is wrung and the bird is stuffed into a compressed cooker, feathers and all.

EPISODE SEVEN: SHE'LL BE COMIN' ROUND THE MOUNTAIN (second suggestion)[11]

1. "She'll be comin' 'round the mountain when she comes" might be used as a warm-up verse.

2. "She'll be driving six white horses when she comes." Select a very attractive girl and have her drive the horses. Give her a flowing, Roman-type garb, with ribbons for lines of the horses, and have six two-person horses, made of a wire framework covered with paper. (This part can be dignified and beautiful if you want it to be.)

3. "We'll kill the old red rooster." With a large, comic card-board axe, take out a red-headed fellow and chop. An improvised head might be used to drop off.

4. "And we'll have chicken and dumplin's when she comes. . . ." A large group come rushing out, seat themselves

11 From Sibley C. Burnett, Nashville, Tenn.

SOME LIKE 'EM WITH MUSIC

at the table (which has been placed there in advance) and make noises of anticipation (or of eating).

5. "We'll all go down to meet her . . ." offers obvious dramatization.

6. "She'll be wearing red pajamas when she comes." She might be wearing a pair of red flannels or long-handled underwear, dyed red . . . and carrying her bag, which one of the boys goes up to take from her.

7. "She will have to sleep with gran'ma when she comes . . ." Have the two of them going to bed, wearing comical costumes.

chapter 7

AN AMUSING STORY

STORY

IS RESTFUL

"cast up by the sea" by stephen leacock
"little david" by roark bradford
"pigs is pigs" by ellis parker butler

AN AMUSING STORY IS RESTFUL

KITS AND STUNTS bring the spirit of fun and enjoyment to a group. Both listener and performer enjoy the
air of spontaneous humor that characterizes good skits and
stunts. But there are situations in which humorous stories are
quite as useful. As breathers after vigorous activity, for those
quiet and relaxing times when the group is just ready to have
someone else supply their fun for them, for a campfire setting, for a home party—in all these situations stories have
been found helpful by many leaders. At the close of some
meeting, particularly one in which there has been tension or
conflict, a twenty-minute period in which people can sit
relaxed and can laugh together over a well-read, amusing
story will prove to be a profitable use of time.

Stephen Leacock's "Cast Up by the Sea" reads almost like
a long skit, and it has many of the same elements as a skit.
(We consider Leacock one of the outstanding modern hu-
morists.) As the script is being read, some of the action here
and there can be made more realistic by an assistant—perhaps serving peanuts to the listeners at the point where they
are sold in the story, or turning the lights in the room up or
down, off or on, as indicated in the script.

"Little David," by Roark Bradford, is included because we
feel that it is a classic of American humor, and because its
genuine folk quality allows the reader and audience to laugh
with, rather than at, these keen insights into human frailty.

Although "Pigs Is Pigs," by Ellis Parker Butler, has been
delighting American audiences for years, its fun is as timely
as ever. It has been selected for reading aloud because of its
basic humor and because it contains much conversation, thus

making it appear to the listener more like a play. For a group ready to settle back and enjoy refreshment as well as refreshments, this story is excellent. It is all the more fun if the group will sit on the floor, and the reader, too. Anyone who has dealt with the red tape of a large corporation will appreciate "Pigs Is Pigs."

"CAST UP BY THE SEA"[1]

A seacoast melodrama—as thrown up for 30 cents—in 1880

BY STEPHEN LEACOCK

Everybody who has reached or passed middle age looks back with affection to that splendid old melodrama, "Cast Up by the Sea." Perhaps it wasn't called exactly that. I believe it was played under forty different names in fifty different forms, but it was always the same good old melodrama of the New England coast, with the farmhouse and the yellow fields running down to the sea, and the lighthouse right at the end of the farm with rocks and the sea beyond, looking for trouble.

For thirty cents you got a thrill from "Cast Up by the Sea" that lasted for twenty years. You had an orchestra chair on the ground floor where you could sit and eat peanuts and study the program till the play began. After it had begun you couldn't eat any more; you were too excited!

The first thing everybody used to do in studying the program was to see how many years elapsed between acts. In those days everybody used to go out between the acts for air. The more years that elapsed and the more acts there were, the more air they could get.

Nobody had yet invented that system of marking the characters "in order of their appearance." You had to try and learn the whole lot before the play began. You would just get

---

[1] Reprinted, by permission of Dodd, Mead & Company, Inc., from *Laugh with Leacock*. Copyright, 1923, 1930, by Dodd, Mead & Company, Inc.

started when up went the curtain with a long, stately roll, two men at the side hoisting it, and there you were looking at the farmstead by the sea.

Notice how quick and easy and attractive that old-fashioned beginning was. One minute you were eating peanuts and studying the program—and the next minute the play had begun!

There was the farmhouse (or at least the porch and door) at the right hand side of the stage, all bathed in sunlight (yellow gas) and the grass plot and the road in the center, and the yellow wheat (quite a bunch of it) at the left, and the fields reaching back till they hit the painted curtain with the lighthouse and the rocks and the sea. Everybody who looked at that lighthouse knew that there would be something doing with it. Either the heroine would be thrown off it or the hero thrown over it—anyway something good.

For the moment all is peace and sunlight on the seashore farm. Zeke and Rube, the hired men, are cutting the little patch of wheat over at the edge of the stage with scythes. Just imagine it—real wheat, they're actually cutting it. (Upon my word, those stage effects of 1880 were simply wonderful!)

Zeke says, "I swan b'gosh heck b'gosh gum yak! yak!"

Rube answers, "Heck gosh b'gum yes, yak! yak!" Both laugh.

These words are meaningless, merely a symbol of New England dialect, farm life, and honesty of character. Presently Rube quits reaping and says,

"So Miss Hope'll be coming back this morning."

"Yes, sir, that she will. A whole year at boarding school. She'll be a growed up lady now, all right."

"Yes sir, and purty as a pitcher, I'll be bound, by heck!"

They whet their scythes with a clang and out comes Martha, the farmer's wife, and Phoebe, the help. With them is a freckled boy who is in all melodramas. His business is to get his ears boxed, mislay the will, lose the mortgage, and otherwise mix up the plot.

"Do you see the buggy coming yet, Zeke?" (Zeke and Rube hop around making gestures of looking down the road, hands up over their eyes.)

"There they are," calls Phoebe, "coming along down in the hollow."

There is great excitement at once. Martha cries, "Land's sakes, if it ain't Hope all right," and boxes the freckled boy's ears. The others run to and fro saying, "Here they come!" so as to get the audience worked up with excitement. At the height of it comes the actual clatter of horse's hoofs and a real horse and buggy drive onto the stage. (That clattering horse coming on to the stage was always one of the great effects in 1880—a real horse with a real harness, and with added anxiety for fear the horse would misbehave himself when he came on.)

The buggy stops with a lot of shouting of "Whoa there"— intended to keep the horse lively. If they didn't shout at it this stage horse was apt to subside into a passive melancholy not suited for the drama.

So here is the farmer sitting in the buggy in a suit of store clothes and a black slouch hat. Beside him is Hope, his daughter. How sweet she looks in her New England sun hat with the flowers on it!

Hope leaps out in one spring and kisses her mother in one bound and she cries, "Well, mother! Well, Phoebe! Well, Zeke! Why, Rube!" They all circulate and hop and dance about saying, "Well, Miss Hope, well, I never!"

You would think that the old homestead represented the high water mark of happiness. But wait a bit. Before long they'll start trouble enough. All the audience know in advance that the farm will be mortgaged and the farmer ruined and Hope driven from home. Trouble was the proper business of melodrama. So presently they all get through congratulations, and Hope goes away to see the brindle cow with the freckled boy, and all fade off the stage except the farmer and his wife. The tone changes.

"Hiram," Martha says, "Lawyer Ellwood's agent was here this morning. He wants his money."

"Ay! he wants his money, does he? Curse him!" The farmer scowls.

"Oh, Hiram, we can't never pay it." Martha puts her apron up to her face and sobs.

"Curse him!" he rages. "Curse him! This three years he has thrown a blight across our life."

"You was friends oncet, Hiram," sobs Martha. "Before he went to the city you was friends."

"Yes, that was before I signed this and signed that and till he thought all was mortgaged away and he held me in the hollow of his hand. If that man stood here now I could choke him with these hands."

Hiram's gesture is so terrible and passionate that it is the one hope of the audience in the top gallery that Lawyer Ellwood will happen along right now and get choked. "But I can pay, Martha. I can throw the money in his face tomorrow. Look, Martha, there it is!" He slaps down a wallet.

"Oh, Hiram!"

"It will mean hard times again, hard and bitter times. . . ."

"I don't mind that, Hiram"—and Martha puts her hands up to her husband's neck—"we've borne it together before and we can bear it again. But oh, Hiram, if only our boy Jack had been spared to us . . ." Martha cries.

"There, there, Martha," says the farmer. "The sea has taken him, Mother, as it has taken many a brave lad before him. . . . But come, Mother, into the house. We mustn't show sad faces for Hope's homecoming. Come. . . ."

The play is getting too sad, so it has to be relieved. Rube and Phoebe go through one of those rural love scenes that were used to ease the strain of the melodrama. Rube, evidently proposing to kiss her, says:

"Ain't you got nothing for me this morning, Phoebe?" And Phoebe says,

"Go along, you big thing, I've got that for you," and swats him over the face with a thistle. The audience roars and the strain is removed. Phoebe disappears with Rube in pursuit.

"Why, Mother"—it is Hope calling—"where are you, Mother?"

"I'm here, daughter," says Martha, reappearing out on the porch.

Hope comes over coyly. "I have been wanting so much to talk to you all by ourselves." Martha has taken Hope's hand in hers and is patting it, and Hope is looking at the ground and swinging herself about on one heel in the way that in a New England play always symbolized the approach of love.

"I think I can guess what it's about. Tell me all about it," says the farmer's wife.

"You remember, Mother, that I wrote and told you that I had a secret—"

"I suppose it means that there is someone . . . that my little girl . . . " (Martha whispers into Hope's ear).

"Oh, Mother," Hope goes on, "it's even greater than that. Look, Mother, see what's on my hand."

Hope holds out her hand, and even the girls in the gallery can see the plain gold ring on her finger. The men in the audience don't get it, but the girls and women explain to them what it is.

"Why, Hope, darling," says Martha, all in a tremble, "what does it mean?"

"It means—it means," Hope takes a flying leap into Mother's arms, "that I'm married."

"Married!"

"Last Saturday in Boston at eleven o'clock in the morning. I couldn't tell you. It all came so sudden. I did so want you there, only it couldn't be. It was in such a hurry because Ned was offered a new ship. Just think, Mother, captain of a ship at twenty-one."

"Don't tell me that your man is a sailor," says Martha Haycroft in evident agitation.

"Why, yes, Mother," says Hope.

"The sea, the sea," groans the farmer's wife. "When will it give me back my boy?"

"There, Mother, you mustn't cry. Ned will be at sea only a little while longer now—just one voyage in the schooner *Good Hope* . . . it's named after me . . . and then he will settle down on a farm beside the sea. His father is a rich lawyer in Boston, Mother, and Ned says that he has a mortgage on a farm right on the seashore just like this and after this one voyage . . ."

"A lawyer, a rich lawyer!"

"Yes, mother, Lawyer Ephraim Ellwood." Martha breaks from daughter in alarm.

At that moment the farmer, Hiram Haycroft, steps on the stage.

"Why, Mother, why Hope! What's all this?"

"I don't know, Father; I began to tell Mother a secret . . . that I'm . . . married, Father."

Hiram comes over affectionately and takes Hope's two hands. "Who's the lucky man who is going to take my little girl?"

All the audience waits in a luxury of expectation. They know that the farmer is going to get an awful jolt. Then he gets it.

"He's the son of a rich Boston lawyer, Father, who—has a mortgage on a farm—"

The farmer has dropped Hope's hands, his face is darkening.

"And Ned is to have the farm—Ned Ellwood is his name, Father. See it here on my marriage certificate?" She timidly takes out a paper.

"Ellwood, Lawyer Ellwood! By the living God, Hope, sooner than see you married to a son of his, I'd see you lying fathoms deep under the sea beside my son! God hears me say it, and may God so order it!"

The curtain slowly falls, and Act I is over.

There is great sadness over the audience because they know from experience that once the old homestead starts going to pieces like this, things will go from bad to worse. Even the fact that the orchestra is now playing "In the Gloaming, Oh, My Darling" doesn't help much.

Presently the men have come back and the orchestra is stopped and the gas cut down and the curtain is hauled away up to the roof and it's—

ACT II. Same Evening. The Kitchen of the
Haycroft Farm.

"You'll find us plain folk, sir, just plain folk. But if it'll please you to take what plain folk can offer you're heartily welcome. Now then, Phoebe girl, a chair here for the gentleman. Put another stick in the stove, Rube, it's a cold night in this November wind."

The stranger, in a strange voice, "Ay, it's a cold night."

The scene is in the farm kitchen, one of those big old farm kitchens of 1880 that filled the whole stage. All eyes of the audience are turned on the stranger. He has a crop of straight white hair (a wig evidently) and a white beard—false, of course—and he walks partly bent with a stick, and he looks around the room with such a queer look, as if he recognized it.

All the audience feel instinctively that that stranger is disguised. In this sort of play there always had to be somebody who turned out to be somebody else.

"I've just been down to the shore, sir," the farmer goes on, "I tend the light here at the foot of the farm. 'Twill be a bad night at sea tonight."

"A bad night for those at sea," repeats the stranger. The wind howls again, and Martha looks up from cooking to say, "The sea, the sea."

"But come, come," says the farmer, "this ain't no night for feeling downhearted. I hear the neighbors outside. Come, Martha, we'll go out and bring them in." They depart, leaving the stranger lost in thought.

Rube and Phoebe do another love scene. He tries to take her around the waist and she lands him across the face with a pancake, and the audience roars with delight until they suddenly come to a full stop when they see that something is happening with the stranger.

Suddenly, without turning his back, he speaks in a loud, clear, young voice: "Rube." Plucking away his white wig and beard he stands revealed.

"Jack! It's Mr. Jack come back from the dead!" cries Phoebe.

"Ain't you drownded?" cries Rube. They crowd close to him in eager recognition and Jack, young and boyish now, laughs and greets them.

"Let me run and call the boss and the missus," pleads Phoebe, but Jack restrains her. "Not now. They mustn't know yet." Then he explains in whispers and gestures and takes from his pocket a bundle of something—is it paper or money or what? Then he redisguises himself in a minute.

There is a loud banging at the door. Rube goes to it and opens it—with a special biff of wind produced for his benefit—and then shows in two strangers, a young man and an old.

The young man is tall and bronzed and sailorlike, and Hope rushes in and with a glad cry of "Ned! My Ned!" throws herself into his arms. In a moment everybody knows that he is her husband.

"We've put in under the point," Ned explains, "and I came ashore. But it's only to say good-bye. The Good Hope can't lie there in this rising wind. We'll have to put off at once. This is my father, Hope. You'll be a daughter to him while I'm gone!"

Hope goes up to the old man and puts her two hands in his and says, oh, so sweetly, "I will indeed, sir, for Ned's sake."

Her mother, who has seen and heard all, shrinks from her place.

"Ellwood," she says, "Lawyer Ellwood."

At that moment the door swings open and Hiram Haycroft, shaking the wet from his black oilskins, strides back into the room. Hope comes to him pleadingly. "Father, Father dear, this is my husband—"

But he doesn't see her. He is staring at Ellwood, trembling.

"You! You that have sought to bring ruin upon me and mine!"

"Hiram," says Ellwood, raising a protesting hand.

"Out before I lay hands on you." Hiram Haycroft reaches for the gun above the mantel. "Out of my house, I say."

The father and son move to the door. Hope rushes to her husband.

"Father, he is my husband! Where he goes I go. Out into the world, for better or for worse. Where you go I follow, my place is at your side."

There is a burst of applause from the audience at this sentiment. That was the kind of girl they raised in 1880. There are none of them now.

The door closes after them. There is a hush and a silence. Martha goes tearfully upstairs, lamp in hand, and Hiram Haycroft sits alone. He sits with head in hands, then goes over to the dresser and takes out the wallet that has his two thousand dollars, holds it a moment and replaces it.

At intervals the storm is heard outside. The audience knows by instinct that there is still more tragedy to come.

The farmer rises slowly from his chair. He lays aside his

oilskins. Then still slowly, he takes off his boots—with a bootjack—a stage effect much valued in melodrama.

He moves about the room, a candle in his hand, bolts and chains the door, and so, step by step, slowly and with much creaking, ascends the stairs to bed.

There is deep silence and waiting. You can hear the audience breathing. No one speaks.

Then a side door opens cautiously and a dark figure steals over to the wallet. Is he taking it, or moving it? Is he a thief or what?

Then suddenly the farmer's voice comes from the landing.

"Who's that? Who's that, I say? Stand there, or I'll shoot." Then the flash of fire and the roar of the gun and the crouching figure falls to the floor.

"Lights here. Bring a light! A thief!" cries the farmer.

Rube holds a light so that the audience can see the pale face—but something has long since told them who it is. There is a loud cry as the farmer's wife sinks down beside the body.

"Jack, Jack, it's my boy come back to me."

And the farmer, the gun still clenched and smoking in his hand, cries:

"My son! I have killed my son!"

And with that down sinks the somber curtain on a silent audience.

That's the way, you see, that the drama was put over in 1880. We weren't afraid of real effects—terror, agony, murder —anything, and the more the better. The farmer is ruined, he's driven his daughter from the door and shot his son— and there you are.

When the play reaches this point, at the end of Act Two, there is nothing for it but a two-years' wait. So the play bill at this point bears the legend "Two Years Elapse Between Acts Two and Three." The audience is glad of it. Without that they couldn't have stood the tragedy of it. The gas is turned up now and the audience are gradually recovering; a boy comes down the aisle and shouts "Peanuts!" That helps a lot. And presently when the orchestra begins to play "My Mother Said That I Never Should," they begin to get reconciled to life again. Anyway, being used to this type of play, they know that things aren't so bad as they seem. Jack can't really be dead. He'll be brought to life somehow. So they look at their programs with a revived interest to see what happens next.

ACT III. Two Years Later. The Fore Shore After
Sunset. A Gathering Storm.

Ah! Look at the scene as the curtain goes up now. Isn't it grand! The rocks and the breaking water and the white foam in the twilight! How ever do they do it? And the lighthouse there at the right-hand side, how it towers into the dark sky! Look at the fishermen all in black oilskins and sou'westers, glistening in the wet, moving about on the shore and pointing to the sea.

Notice that short flash of yellow lightning and the rumble of thunder away behind the scene. And look at the long beams of the light from the lighthouse far out on the water.

"A wild night!" It was a fisherman speaking—no, it's Rube, only you would hardly know him—all in oilskins. Zeke, another fisherman, says:

"It's all that! God help all poor souls out at sea to-night."

The lightning and thunder make good again, the fishermen and the women on shore move to and fro, talking and excited, and pointing at the sea. Rube and Zeke come together in the foreground, talking.

Soon the audience notices Jack with a queer, strange, blank look on his face. He is holding to his mother.

"Jack, come home, Jack! It's no place for you here in the storm."

Jack turns a vacant countenance upon his mother and the

audience gets it. He has been speechless and demented for these two years since he was shot. He points toward the waves with wild, growing excitement.

"He has a sailor's eyes. What does he see?"

"A ship! A ship! There's a vessel out on the reef. See! Look!"

They run up and down, pointing and shouting. And far out on the waves, lit for a moment by a flash of lightning, the audience can see a dismasted schooner—she's made of cardboard—out beside the breakers on the reef.

At this moment the freckled boy, all in oilskins, rushes breathless on to the stage. He hasn't grown an inch in two years, but nobody cares about that.

"Mother, Rube," he gasps. "I've been down to the Long Point—I ran all the way—there's a schooner going on the reef. Mother, it's the *Good Hope*."

"The *Good Hope?*" exclaims everybody.

"They were lowering the boats . . . but nothing can live in that sea . . . one boat went down and I could see Hope standing by the mast. We've got to get the lifeboats. We've got to go. You men, who'll come?"

Come! They'll all come! Listen to the shouts of them. See! They are dragging forth the lifeboat from its wooden house on the left of the stage. There are swinging lanterns and loud calls and the roaring of the wind. The stage is darkening and the lightning glares on the sea.

"Look—a boat! a boat! Out there on the reef, right among the breakers."

"Mother, Mother, it's Hope. She's alone in the boat, she's kneeling, she's praying."

One of the fishermen cries out, "There's only one man can pilot this boat across that reef, only Hiram Haycroft."

There are cries of "Hiram! Hiram!" They point out at the lighthouse from which the long beams still revolve on the water. "He can't leave the light."

"He must leave the light."

"It's life or death on this one chance. Lads, stand ready there with the lifeboat and come, some of you with me to bring him down." They rush toward the lighthouse. There is noise and thunder; a flash of lightning shows the boat right among the breakers. Hope is seen for a moment kneeling in the bow and praying, her face illuminated in the lightning. Then in a swirl of white water the boat vanishes in the foam of the reef!

ACT IV

Then the scene changes—all done in a minute—from the shore to the Lighthouse Tower. It is what used to be called a "transformation scene." It involved an eclipse of darkness punctured by little gas jets, a terrible thumping and bumping with an undertone of voices. You could hear a voice in the darkness say distinctly, "Get that blank blank drop over there," and you could see black figures running round in the transformation. Then there came an awful crash and a vision of a black curtain sliding down amongst the dark men. The lights flicked up again and all the audience broke into applause at the final wonder of it.

Look! It's the lighthouse tower with the big lights burning and the storm howling outside. How bright and clear it is here inside the tower with its great windows looking out over the storm sixty feet above the sea.

"God help all poor souls at sea tonight," says Hiram as he looks out the window. A rush of feet brings the group of fishermen, Martha and Jack, crowding into the lighthouse tower. Jack, at the rear of all, has a light of new intelligence on his face.

"Quick, Hiram, you must come. There has been a wreck and a boat's going on the reef."

"My place is here," he says.

"Hiram, it's the Good Hope that was wrecked, and the boat drifting . . . it's Hope, it's our daughter," pleads Martha. Hiram staggers back against the wall, but his voice is firm.

"Martha, I'm sworn to tend the light. If the light fails, God knows what it means to the ships at sea. If my child is lost it is God's will—but—my place is here." He turns back to the light.

Suddenly Jack steps into the center of the floor.

"Father, Mother," he says, "I'll save her. Give me the rope."

He points to a long coil of rope against the wall and with the end of the line around his body, he throws open the door and rushes on the iron platform. "Hold fast to the line," he calls, and then the audience sees him mount the iron rail, pause a moment, then dive head first into the sea beneath.

There is shouting and clamor from the fishermen.

"There he is! Look, he's swimming to her! Hold fast there! He's got her. . . . Now then, in with the line."

And with one glorious haul, up comes the line from the roaring sea with Jack at the end of it and, tight held in his encircling arms, the fainting form of Hope, his sister.

Couldn't be done? Nonsense! That was nothing to what we used to see done in the old-time plays. If need be, Jack could have fished out a whole shipload!

There is a cry of "Saved, saved!" and Hiram Haycroft, clasping the senseless form of his daughter to his heart, cries,

"My little gal! Cast up by the sea!"

And the curtain comes down to a roar of applause.

ACT V. Six Months Later. Scene. The Kitchen of the
Haycroft Farm.

This last act in the melodrama is all to the good. There is no more tragedy, no strain, no trouble. The play is really over, but this part is always put in as a sort of wind-up to make everybody happy. The audience is now sitting in a swim of luxurious sentimentality.

How fine everything has turned out—Jack got his mind back, and Hope is saved and her husband too, and the old farm isn't mortgaged or sold, and the Haycrofts are not ruined after all. Yes, and more than that: there are all kinds of little items of happiness to be thrown in.

Here we are back in the old farm kitchen and here, of course, are Rube and Phoebe again. And Rube tries to grab Phoebe round the waist but she says, "Oh, you Rube, you go along," and lands a dish towel in his face. But this time Rube won't go along! He catches Phoebe and tells her that he wants her to be his wife and throw dishcloths at him all his life, and Phoebe calls him a "big thing" and gives him a kiss like a smack (worse than a dishcloth or a pancake).

In come the farmer, and his son Jack, and Ned, Hope's husband. The farmer seems very old and infirm, though suffused with the same air of peace and happiness as all the others. The two young men help him into an arm rocking chair. "Easy now." Then Hiram sits down with that expression of difficulty, "Ay-ee-ee," always used to symbolize stage rheumatism. There is really no need for the farmer to become so suddenly old in the last act, but it was a favorite custom of 1880 to make all the old people very infirm and very happy at the end of the play.

So they begin to talk, just to pile on the happiness.

"I'm getting old, lads, I'm not the man I was."

"Old, Father!" laughs Jack. "Why, you're the youngest and spryest of all of us—"

"I'm getting past work, boys," says the farmer, shaking his head, "past work—"

Then it develops that Jack is going to work the place and tend the light, and Ned, Hope's husband, is to be on the farm adjoining, and that he and Hope are ready to move in just as soon as—

But wait a minute.

Ned's father! Lawyer Ellwood. And the terrible feud!

Oh, pshaw, just watch that feud vanish! In the fifth act of an old-time melodrama a feud could be blown to the four winds like thistledown.

Like this:

There's a knocking at the door. Ned goes to it, comes back all smiling and says:

"There's someone at the door to see you, Mr. Haycroft. An old friend, he says. Shall he come in?"

"An old friend?" And in slips Ellwood—the farmer's enemy, Hope's father-in-law—looking pretty hale and hearty, but with the same touch of the old age of the fourth act visible. He comes over and says,

"Well, Hiram, have you a shake of the hand for an old friend?"

"Why, Ephraim, it's not your hand I should be taking; it's your forgiveness I ought to be asking for my mad folly these two years past."

And what do you think! He'd been Hiram's friend all along and was not in earnest about wanting the money back from Hiram—didn't want it at all! He knew about Hope's love affair and Jack's safe return with his son and was tickled to death over it—and that night two years ago when the farmer drove him out he had come over to tell the Haycrofts that the debt was cancelled, and he was going to buy a farm and start the young people, Ned and Hope, in life— and it was the cancelled mortgage that Jack was trying to sneak over and put in the drawer when his father shot him down!—and—why, dear me, how simple it all is in the fifth act!

Why didn't he explain? Why didn't he shout, "Hiram, I'm not a villain at all, I'm your old friend—" Oh, pshaw, who ever did explain things in the second act of a melodrama?

So they are still explaining and getting happier and happier when the last climax is staged.

The audience hears Martha's voice as she comes on stage, talking back into the wings, "Carry him carefully there, Phoebe, for the land's sake, if you drop that precious child—" And in they come.

Martha—and Hope! Looking as sweet and fresh as when she started out years ago in the first act. And bringing up the rear is Phoebe—carrying the baby.

Yes, believe it or not, a baby!—or the very semblance of one all bundled up in white. Hope's baby! No melodrama was ever brought to its righteous end without a baby.

How the women all cuddle round it and croon over it! They put it on the farmer's lap—and say, isn't he just clumsy when he tries to take it—and when Rube offers to help and Phoebe slaps his face with a dishrag, the audience just goes into fits of laughter.

So there you are—and everybody saved. All happy, the baby installed on the farmer's knees, and explanations flowing like autumn cider.

All that is needed now is for the farmer to get off the Final Religious Sentiment which is the end and benediction of the good old melodrama. So he utters it with all due solemnity: "Ay, lads, pin your hope in Providence and in the end you land safe in port." It sounds as convincing as a proposition in Euclid!

Then the curtain slowly comes down and the matinee audience melts away, out in the murky November evening, with the flickering gas lamps in the street and the clanging bells of the old horsecars in their ears, but with their souls uplifted and illuminated with the moral glow of the melodrama.

"LITTLE DAVID"[2]

BY ROARK BRADFORD

Well, de Hebrews whupped de Philistines and de Philistines whupped de Hebrews. But neither side wouldn't stay whupped. So finally de Lawd sort of got tired stayin' round to he'p out de Hebrews all de time, so he app'inted a man name King Saul to be kind er de Hebrews.

"King Saul," say de Lawd, "you take and lead my people while I go on back and 'tend to my angels a little."

Ole King Saul was a purty good king when hit come to fightin', but when hit come to jest plain ev'yday kingin', old Saul wa'n't so much. But as long as he whupped de Philistines de people hung wid him, and sort of put up wid him for de rest er de time. So Saul started to think he was purty good all de way round.

"What a king needs," say ole King Saul, "is a heap er music round de camp." So he sont out and got a little boy name Little David to come and play on his harp round de camp.

Little David was one er deseyar boys which could do mighty nigh anything and could do hit good. But when hit come right down to hit, he could make up songs and sing 'em better'n he could do anything else. He always was makin' up a song and playin' hit on his harp and singin'. Even while he was out herdin' his daddy's sheep he'd take and put his harp in his pocket and set out on de hillside and sing:

"Ef I could I sholy would,
 I wanter stand on de rocks whar Moses stood.
 Little David, play on yo' harp, hallelu! hallelu!
 Little David, play on yo' harp, hallelu!"

[2] Reprinted, by permission of Mrs. Roark Bradford, Santa Fe, New Mexico, from *Ol' Man Adam an' His Chillun* by Roark Bradford (New York: Harper and Brothers. 1932).

So while he was singin' a big bear come and stole a sheep and he had to git up and run de bear down to git de sheep back. Den he went on back and sung some mo':

> "Old Joshua was de son of Nun,
>   And he never quit fightin' to de fightin' was done.
>   Little David, play on yo' harp, hallelu! hallelu!
>   Little David, play on yo' harp, hallelu!"

So 'bout dat time yar come a line and stole another sheep, so Little David had to git up and run him down.

"Dis ain't gittin' nowheres," he say. "I'm gittin' sick and tired er runnin' deseyar thievin' varmints down ev'y time they steals a sheep. I bet I'm gonter fix me somethin' which'll do my runnin' for me." So he tuck and cut de tongue outer his shoe and got two strings and make him a slingshot. So he set down and started singin' again:

> "Old Joshua stood on de top er de hill,
>   And he looked at de sun and de sun stood still.
>   Little David, play on yo' harp, hallelu! hallelu!
>   Little David, play on yo' harp, hallelu!"

So 'bout dat time a wolf came up and steal hisse'f a sheep. But David didn't git up and run after him. He jest got a rock and put hit in de slingshot and slung hit round his head about twice, and ker-blip! de wolf thought de lightnin' had done struck him!

So when ole King Saul sont for Little David, Little David not only tuck 'long his harp, but he tuck 'long his slingshot, too. So one day he was settin' out in front of ole King Saul's tent, playin' and singin' away to all at once hit started to get dark and de yearth started to tremble and de ground started to shake.

"What dat, ole King Saul?" say Little David.

"Dat's ole Goliar," say ole King Saul.

"Who he?" say David.

"De he-man er de Philistines," say King Saul.

"What do he want?" say David.

"Trouble," say ole King Saul.

"Well, you de king, ain't you?" say Little David. "Can't you ease his worries 'long dat line?"

"Who, me?" say Saul. "I'm a married man. Cou'se I ain't skeered of him, but still and at de same time I got a wife and a family dependin' on me for s'port. So I don't see no reason how come I should git out and git hurted by no gi'nt."

"He's a gi'nt?" say Little David.

"Twenty foot tall," say King Saul.

"What else is he?" say David.

"Jest wait to he gits out in de clearin' and starts makin' his say-so," say King Saul.

So 'bout dat time ole Goliar stepped out in de clearin' and commenced makin' his say-so.

"I'm a cross betwixt a wild cat and de yaller ianders," he say. "I'm sired by Trouble and dammed by Sudden Death. I drinks nothin' but stump water, and a rattlesnake bit me and died. I breathes out forked lightnin' and I spits out thunder. When I laughs de skies pop open, and when I groans hit rolls up like a ball er yarn. I kills my friends and I makes hamburgers outer my enemies. Tornadoes and harrycanes follow me round like pet dogs, and lines and tigers is my playmates. I'm bad. I'm mean. I'm vicious, and jest natchally can't he'p it. When I gits sick hit takes nothin' less'n a Hebrew man's meat to cyore me. And I feel a buck auger comin' on. So look out! I'm reekin' wid meanness and I'm huntin' trouble."

"Sounds hard, don't he?" say Little David.

"Sounds?" say ole King Saul. "Son, dat big scound'el *is* hard!"

"Is you skeered of him?" say Little David.

"Naw, I ain't skeered of him," say ole King Saul, "'cause I got sense enough to keep out'n his way."

"I ain't skeered of him," say Little David.

"You kin run purty fast, kin you?" say Saul.

"Naw, I ain't de runnin' kind," say Little David. "I'm jest goin' up yonder and whup dat scound'el befo' supper time."

"You gonter which?" say ole King Saul.

"I'm gonter whup him," say Little David, "or else he gonter whup me."

"Well," say ole King Saul, "be keerful and don't meet up wid de old Fool Killer on yo' way over, 'cause efn de Fool Killer meet up with you, he gonter beat ole Goliar to you."

Little David didn't said a word. He jest tuck his harp in one hand and his slingshot in de yuther, and went off singin':

"When I gits to heaven I' gonter be like Job.
I'm gonter wawk all around in my long white robe.
Little David, play on yo' harp, hallelu! hallelu!
Little David, play on yo' harp, hallelu!"

So when ole Goliar seed Little David he say, "What you doin' over yar on my side, little old Hebrew boy?"

"I thought I yared somebody say you was lookin' for trouble," say Little David.

"Don't play wid me, little boy," say Goliar. "I'm in a bad humor and I ain't kilt me no Hebrew since yistiddy. Trot 'long back home befo' I gits mad and spatters you up ag'in' de side er de yearth."

"You don't want to fight wid me?" say Little David. "I yared 'bout deseyar boys wid de big say-so, and fum what I yars, hit's all say-so and no do-so."

Well, dat made old Goliar good and hot, so he arch up his back and squunch down his shoulders and start stifflaigin' round and roarin' and bellowin.' "I'm comin', so jest watch out for me," he say. "I'm dealin' death and destruction right yar and now." And he danced stiff-laigged round Little

David, jest groanin' and gruntin' like hit's hurtin' him pow-
erful bad to hold hisse'f back to he gits done wid his dancin'
and tawkin'.

"I'm comin', 'cause I can't hold myse'f back no longer,"
say ole Goliar and he started tward Little David.

So Little David jest drap a rock into his slingshot and
slung hit round his head, and ker-plop! he tuck ole Goliar
right between de eyes and ole Goliar never knowed what
hit him.

So 'bout dat time de Lawd stepped out f'm behind a bush
and say: "Well, dat settles hit, Little David. You gonter be
king over my people."

"Aw, Lawd," say Little David, "ole King Saul is de king."

"You mean he was de king," say de Lawd. "I been holdin'
on to him 'cause he makes out like he can fight. But you not
on'y kin sing, but you kin outfight him, too, and ev'ybody
knows ole King Saul can't sing. So hit's jest like I say, son.
You de king, and no argyment wid me 'bout hit."

"Well, thanky, Lawd," say Little David. So he picks up
his harp and wawked on back to camp, singin':

> "Little David was a shepherd's boy,
> And he killed ole Goliar and he hollered wid joy.
> Little David, play on yo' harp, hallelu! hallelu!
> Little David, play on yo' harp, hallelu!"

"PIGS IS PIGS"[3]

BY ELLIS PARKER BUTLER

Mike Flannery, the Westcote agent of the Interurban Express Company, leaned over the counter of the express office
and shook his fist. Mr. Morehouse, angry and red, stood on
the other side of the counter, trembling with rage. The
argument had been long and heated, and at last Mr. More-

---

[3] Copyright, 1905, by Ellis Parker Butler. Reprinted with the permission
of Harold Ober Associates.

house had talked himself speechless. The cause of the
trouble stood on the counter between the two men. It was
a soapbox, across the top of which were nailed a number of
strips, forming a rough but serviceable cage. In it two
spotted guinea pigs were greedily eating lettuce leaves.

"Do as you loike, then!" shouted Flannery, "pay for thim
an' take thim, or don't pay for thim and leave thim be. Rules
is rules, Misther Morehouse, an' Mike Flannery's not goin'
to be called down fer breakin' of thim."

"But, you everlastingly stupid idiot!" shouted Mr. Morehouse, madly shaking a flimsy printed book beneath the
agent's nose, "can't you read it here—in your own plain
printed rates? 'Pets, domestic, Franklin to Westcote, if
properly boxed, twenty-five cents each.'" He threw the
book on the counter in disgust. "What more do you want?
Aren't they pets? Aren't they domestic? Aren't they properly
boxed? What?"

He turned and walked back and forth rapidly, frowning
ferociously.

Suddenly he turned to Flannery and, forcing his voice to
an artificial calmness, spoke slowly but with intense sarcasm.

"Pets," he said "P-e-t-s! Twenty-five cents each. There are
two of them. One! Two! Two times twenty-five are fifty! Can
you understand that? I offer you fifty cents."

Flannery reached for the book. He ran his hand through
the pages and stopped at page sixty-four.

"An' I don't take fifty cints," he whispered in mockery.
"Here's the rule for ut. 'Whin the agint be in anny doubt
regardin' which of two rates applies to a shipment, he shall
charge the larger. The consign-ey may file a claim for the
overcharge.' In this case, Misther Morehouse, I be in doubt.
Pets thim animals may be, an' domestic they may be, but
pigs I'm blame sure they do be, an' me rules says plain as
the nose on yer face, 'Pigs, Franklin to Westcote, thirty cints

each.' An' Mister Morehouse, by me arithmetical knowledge two times thirty comes to sixty cints."

Mr. Morehouse shook his head savagely. "Nonsense!" he shouted, "confounded nonsense, I tell you! Why, you poor ignorant foreigner, that rule means common pigs, domestic pigs, not guinea pigs!"

Flannery was stubborn.

"Pigs is pigs," he declared firmly. "Guinea pigs, or Eye-talian pigs or Irish pigs is all the same to the Interurban Express Company an' to Mike Flannery. Th' nationality of the pig creates no differentiality in the rate, Misther More-house! 'Twould be the same was they Dutch pigs or Rooshun pigs. Mike Flannery," he added, "is here to tind to the ex-priss business and not to hould conversation wid pigs in sivinteen languages fer to discover be they Chinese or Tip-perary by birth an' nativity."

Mr. Morehouse hesitated. He bit his lip and then flung out his arms wildly.

"Very well!" he shouted, "you shall hear of this! Your president shall hear of this! It is an outrage! I have offered you fifty cents. You refuse it! Keep the pigs until you are ready to take the fifty cents, but, by George, sir, if one hair of those pigs' heads is harmed I will have the law on you!"

He turned and stalked out, slamming the door. Flannery carefully lifted the soapbox from the counter and placed it in a corner. He was not worried. He felt the peace that comes to a faithful servant who has done his duty and done it well.

Mr. Morehouse went home raging. His boy, who had been awaiting the guinea pigs, knew better than to ask him for them. He was a normal boy and therefore always had a guilty conscience when his father was angry. So the boy slipped quietly around the house. There is nothing so sooth-ing to a guilty conscience as to be out of the path of the avenger.

Mr. Morehouse stormed into the house. "Where's the ink?" he shouted at his wife as soon as his foot was across the doorsill.

Mrs. Morehouse jumped, guiltily. She never used ink, but her husband's tone convicted her of the guilt of having borne and reared a boy, and she knew that whenever her husband wanted anything in a loud voice the boy had been at it.

"I'll find Sammy," she said meekly.

When the ink was found Mr. Morehouse wrote rapidly, and he read the completed letter and smiled a triumphant smile.

"That will settle that crazy Irishman!" he exclaimed. "When they get that letter he will hunt another job, all right!"

A week later Mr. Morehouse received a long official envelope with the card of the Interurban Express Company in the upper left corner. He tore it open eagerly and drew out a sheet of paper. At this top it bore the number A6754.

The letter was short. "Subject—Rate on guinea pigs," it said, "Dr. Sir—We are in receipt of your letter regarding rate on guinea pigs between Franklin and Westcote, addressed to the president of this company. All claims for overcharge should be addressed to the Claims Department."

Mr. Morehouse wrote to the Claims Department. He wrote six pages of choice sarcasm, vituperation, and argument, and sent them to the Claims Department.

A few weeks later he received a reply from the Claims Department. Attached to it was his last letter.

"Dr. Sir," said the reply. "Your letter of the 16th inst., addressed to this Department, subject rate on guinea pigs from Franklin to Westcote, rec'd. We have taken up the matter with our agent at Westcote, and his reply is attached herewith. He informs us that you refused to receive the consignment or to pay the charges. You have therefore no claim

against this company, and your letter regarding the proper
rate on the consignment should be addressed to our Tariff
Department."

Mr. Morehouse wrote to the Tariff Department. He stated
his case clearly, and gave his arguments in full, quoting a
page or two from the encyclopedia to prove that guinea pigs
were not common pigs.

With the care that characterizes corporations when they
are systematically conducted, Mr. Morehouse's letter was
numbered, O.K.'d, and started through the regular channels.
Duplicate copies of the bill of lading, manifest, Flannery's
receipt for the package, and several other pertinent papers
were pinned to the letter, and they were passed to the head
of the Tariff Department.

The head of the Tariff Department put his feet on his
desk and yawned. He looked through the papers carelessly.

"Miss Kane," he said to his stenographer, "take this letter:
'Agent, Westcote, N. J. Please advise why consignment re-
ferred to in attached paper was refused domestic pet rates.'"

Miss Kane made a series of curves and angles on her note-
book and waited with pencil poised. The head of the department looked at the papers again.

"Huh! guinea pigs!" he said. "Probably starved to death
by this time! Add this to that letter: "Give condition of consignment at present.'"

He tossed the papers onto the stenographer's desk, took
his feet from his own desk, and went out to lunch.

When Mike Flannery received the letter he scratched his
head.

"Give prisint condition," he repeated thoughtfully. "Now
what do thim clerks be wantin' to know, I wonder! 'Prisint
condition,' is ut? Thim pigs, praise St. Patrick, do be in
good health, so far as I know, but I niver was no veterinairy
surgeon to pigs. Mebby thim clerks wants me to call in the
pig docther an' have their pulses took. Wan thing I do

know, howiver, which is they've glorious appytites for pigs
their soize. Ate? They'd ate the brass padlocks off a barn
door! If the paddy pig, by the same token, ate as hearty as
these pigs do, there'd be a famine in Ireland."

To assure himself that his report would be up to date,
Flannery went to the rear of the office and looked into the
cage. The pigs had been transferred to a larger box—a dry
goods box.

"Wan, . . . two, . . . t'ree, . . . four, . . . five, . . . six, . . .
sivin, . . . eight!" he counted. "Sivin spotted an' wan all black.
All well an' hearty an' all eatin' loike ragin' hippypotty-
musses." He went back to his desk and wrote.

"Mr. Morgan, Head of Tariff Department," he wrote.
"Why do I say guinea pigs is pigs? Because they is pigs and
will be till you say they ain't which is what the rule book
says stop your jollying me you know it as well as I do. As
to health they are all well and hoping you are the same.
P.S. There are eight now the family increased all good eat-
ers. P.S. I paid out so far two dollars for cabbage which
they like shall I put in bill for same what?"

Morgan, head of the Tariff Department, when he received
this letter, laughed. He read it again and became serious.

"By George!" he said, "Flannery is right, 'pigs is pigs.' I'll
have to get authority on this thing. Meanwhile, Miss Kane,
take this letter: Agent, Westcote, N. J. Regarding shipment
guinea pigs, File No. A6754. Rule 83, General Instructions
to Agents, clearly states that agents shall collect from consignee all costs of provender, etc., etc., required for live stock
while in transit or storage. You will proceed to collect same
from consignee."

Flannery received this letter next morning, and when he
read it he grinned.

"Proceed to collect," he said softly. "How thim clerks do
loike to be talkin'! Me proceed to collect two dollars and
twinty-foive cints off Misther Morehouse! I wonder do

thim clerks know Misther Morehouse? I'll get it! Oh, yes! 'Misther Morehouse, two an' a quarter, plaze.' 'Cert'nly, me dear frind Flannery. Delighted! Not!"

Flannery drove the express wagon to Mr. Morehouse's door. Mr. Morehouse answered the bell.

"Ah, ha!" he cried as soon as he saw it was Flannery. "So you've come to your senses at last, have you? I thought you would! Bring the box in."

"I hev no box," said Flannery coldly. "I hev a bill agin Misther John C. Morehouse for two dollars and twinty-foive cints for kebbages aten by his pigs. Wud you wish to pay ut?"

"Pay—cabbages—!" gasped Mr. Morehouse. "Do you mean to say that two little guinea pigs—"

"Eight!" said Flannery. "Papa an' mamma an' the six childer. Eight!"

For answer Mr. Morehouse slammed the door in Flannery's face. Flannery looked at the door reproachfully.

"I take ut the con-sign-y don't want to pay for them kebbages," he said, "If I know signs of refusal, the con-sign-y refuses to pay for wan dang kebbage leaf an' be hanged to me!"

Mr. Morgan, head of the Tariff Department, consulted the president of the Interurban Express Company regarding guinea pigs, as to whether they were pigs or not pigs. . . . "A thing that can come under two rates is naturally to be classed as the higher. But are guinea pigs, pigs? Aren't they rabbits?"

"Come to think of it," said the president, "I believe they are more like rabbits. Sort of halfway station between pig and rabbit. I think the question is this—are guinea pigs of the domestic pig family? I'll ask Professor Gordon. He is authority on such things. Leave the papers with me."

The president put the papers on his desk and wrote a letter to Professor Gordon. Unfortunately the professor was in South America collecting zoological specimens, and the letter was forwarded to him by his wife. As the professor was in the highest Andes, where no white man had ever penetrated, the letter was many months in reaching him. The president forgot the guinea pigs, Morgan forgot them, Mr. Morehouse forgot them, but Flannery did not. One-half of his time he gave to the duties of his agency; the other half was devoted to the guinea pigs. Long before Professor Gordon received the president's letter Morgan received one from Flannery.

"About them pigs," it said, "what shall I do they are great in family life, no race suicide for them, there are thirty-two now shall I sell them do you take this express office for a menagerie, answer quick."

Morgan reached for a telegraph blank and wrote:

"Agent, Westcote. Don't sell pigs."

He then wrote Flannery a letter calling his attention to the fact that the pigs were not the property of the company but were merely being held during a settlement of a dispute regarding rates. He advised Flannery to take the best possible care of them.

Flannery, letter in hand, looked at the pigs and sighed. The drygoods box cage had become too small. He boarded up twenty feet of the rear of the express office to make a large and airy home for them, and went about his business. He worked with feverish intensity when out on his rounds, for the pigs required attention and took most of his time. Some months later, in desperation, he seized a sheet of paper and wrote "160" across it and mailed it to Morgan. Morgan returned it asking for explanation. Flannery replied:

"There be now one hundred sixty of them pigs, for heavens sake let me sell off some, do you want me to go crazy, what."

"Sell no pigs," Morgan wired.

Not long after this the president of the express company received a letter from Professor Gordon. It was a long and scholarly letter, but the point was that the guinea pig was the *Cavia aparoea* while the common pig was the genus *Sus* of the family *Suidae*. He remarked that they were prolific and multiplied rapidly.

"They are not pigs," said the president, decidedly, to Morgan. "The twenty-five cent rate applies."

Morgan made the proper notation on the papers that had accumulated in File A6754, and turned them over to the Audit Department. The Audit Department took some time to look the matter up, and after the usual delay wrote Flannery that as he had on hand one hundred and sixty guinea pigs, the property of consignee, he should deliver them and collect charges at the rate of twenty-five cents each.

Flannery spent a day herding his charges through a narrow opening in their cage so that he might count them.

"Audit Dept." he wrote, when he had finished the count, "you are way off there may be was one hundred and sixty pigs once, but wake up don't be a back number. I've got even eight hundred, now shall I collect for eight hundred or what, how about sixty-four dollars I paid out for cabbages."

It required a great many letters back and forth before the Audit Department was able to understand why the error had been made of billing one hundred and sixty instead of eight hundred, and still more time for it to get the meaning of the "cabbages."

Flannery was crowded into a few feet at the extreme front of the office. The pigs had all the rest of the room and two boys were employed constantly attending to them. The day after Flannery had counted the guinea pigs there were eight more added to his drove, and by the time the Audit Department gave him authority to collect for eight hundred Flannery had given up all attempts to attend to the re-

ceipts or the delivery of goods. He was hastily building gal-
leries around the express office, tier above tier. He had four
thousand sixty-four guinea pigs to care for. More were arriving daily.

Immediately following its authorization the Audit Department sent another letter, but Flannery was too busy to open
it. They wrote another and then they telegraphed:

"Error in guinea pig bill. Collect for two guinea pigs, fifty
cents. Deliver all to consignee."

Flannery read the telegram and cheered up. He wrote out
a bill as rapidly as his pencil could travel over the paper and
ran all the way to the Morehouse home. At the gate he
stopped suddenly. The house stared at him with vacant eyes.
The windows were bare of curtains and he could see into
the empty rooms. A sign on the porch said, "For Rent." Mr.
Morehouse had not only moved, but he had left Westcote.
Flannery returned to the express office and found that two
hundred and six guinea pigs had entered the world since he
left. He wrote a telegram to the Audit Department.

"Can't collect fifty cents for two guinea pigs consignee
has left town address unknown what shall I do? Flannery."

The telegram was handed to one of the clerks in the Audit
Department, and as he read it he laughed.

"Flannery must be crazy. He ought to know that the thing
to do is to return the consignment here," said the clerk. He
telegraphed Flannery to send the pigs to the main office of
the company at Franklin.

When Flannery received the telegram he set to work. The
six boys he had engaged to help him also set to work. They
worked with the haste of desperate men, making cages out
of soapboxes, cracker boxes, and all kinds of boxes, and as
fast as the cages were completed they filled them with guinea
pigs and expressed them to Franklin. Day after day the cages
of guinea pigs flowed in a steady stream from Westcote to
Franklin, and still Flannery and six helpers ripped and nailed

and packed—relentlessly and feverishly. At the end of the week they had shipped two hundred and eighty cases of guinea pigs, and there were in the express office seven hundred and four more pigs than when they began packing them.

"Stop sending pigs. Warehouses full," came a telegram to Flannery. He stopped packing only long enough to wire back, "Can't stop," and kept on sending them. On the next train up from Franklin came one of the company's inspectors. He had instructions to stop the stream of guinea pigs at all hazards. As his train drew up at Westcote station he saw a cattle-car standing on the express company's siding. When he reached the express office he saw the express wagon backed up to the door. Six boys were carrying bushel baskets full of guinea pigs from the office and dumping them into the wagon. Inside the room Flannery, with his coat and vest off, was shoveling guinea pigs into bushel baskets with a coal scoop. He was winding up the guinea pig episode.

He looked up at the inspector with a snort of anger.

"Wan wagonload more an' I'll be quit of thim, an' niver will ye catch Flannery wid no more foreign pigs on his hands. No, sur! They near was the death o' me. Nixt toime I'll know that pigs of whatever nationality is domistic pets—an' go at the lowest rate."

He began shoveling again rapidly, speaking quickly between breaths.

"Rules may be rules, but you can't fool Mike Flannery twice wid the same trick—whin ut comes to live stock, dang the rules. So long as Flannery runs this expriss office—pigs is pets an' cows is pets—an' horses is pets—an' lions an' tigers an' Rocky Mountain goats is pets—an' the rate on thim is twinty-foive cints."

He paused long enough to let one of the boys put an empty basket in the place of the one he had just filled. There were only a few guinea pigs left. As he noted their limited number his natural habit of looking on the bright side returned.

"Well, annyhow," he said cheerfully, "'tis not so bad as ut might be. What if thim foreign pigs had been elephants!"

chapter 8

CAN

YOU

DO

THIS?

feats
forfeits and initiation stunts

WHEN IT IS TIME for initiations, or when the group are just standing around, or when they are sitting at the table between courses, often it is fun to have a filler to demonstrate or suggest.

Here is a variety of physical feats, tricks, easy contests of skill, to fit into those very situations and many others. Many would be good at parties. This section has much material especially designed for boys and men.

Go through the entire section and mark those which appeal to you.

FEATS

Balance the Feather

Can you balance a feather on your nose?

Throw Ping-Pong Ball

Can you throw a ping-pong ball the greatest distance? Measure distance for each player.

Curving Ping-Pong Ball

If you throw a ping-pong ball hard with a straight, forward motion, but let it roll off the forefinger and middle finger, the ball will curve upward, especially near the end of its flight.

Swing the Bell

Can you swing a bell without ringing it?

Candle Blow

Set up candles in any formation—square, circle, triangle— and from a given distance see who can blow out the most.

Squeezing Seeds

When served watermelon or other melon, see who can snap or squeeze seeds and make them go the greatest distance. (Don't forget to make "watermelon false teeth" from the rinds! Just cut out some outlandish teeth and insert in the mouth between lip and gums.)

Swat Him

With a swatter made from a cloth-stuffed sock, each of the two opponents tries to swat the other while in a burlap sack.

Blindfold Swat

Same idea as Swat Him, but each person is blindfolded. The group will enjoy this.

Find the Clock

Blindfold a person and see how long it takes him to find a hidden clock. Have several contestants, keep them out of the area where the clock is to be hidden, hide the clock in the same place every time, bring them in one at a time to try their luck. A watch with a second hand records the time required for each person.

Who Touched Me?

When a player is blindfolded, have him guess who touched him, or who made that noise.

Friendly Blindfold

Have two persons, blindfolded, try to walk up to each other and shake hands. Try many pairs in the group to see if they can do it.

Big Hold

See how many beans you can hold between your fingers. See who in the entire group can hold the most.

Testing Water

The prospectors were searching for fresh water. (Go on with the story.) They did not want to taste it, for they would become thirstier if it were salt water. So they tested it the way I am going to. (Have some glasses of salt water and fresh water brought out. You can indicate the salt water because an egg floats in it but sinks in the fresh.)

Sweetness and Lye

Have two matches representing a boy and a girl. Indicate that a touch of lye (soap) on the water on which the matches are floating, will turn them away from each other, but a bit of sugar will make them come together.

Making a Glass Sing

Tempered glass of the cut-glass variety will usually "sing" if you will wet your finger and run it around the rim.

Touch Floor Backward

Can you stand, bend backward, and touch the floor with your hands?

Jumping, Feet to Hands

Can you jump continuously from feet to hands, alternately spreading and closing your feet and hands?

Circles

Can you make circles with the right hand on the table in one direction and with a foot on the floor in an opposite direction?

Tricky Writing

Can you move beans from one circle on the table to another with one hand and write your name with the other?

Hop and Turn

Can you place one foot against the wall, then hop over it with the other foot, doing a half-turn in the process?

Hopping Hats

Have a row of hats. Each person hops over the first one forward, second backward, and so on, picking last hat up in mouth and tossing it backward overhead.

Stand a Minute

Can you balance for a full minute on one foot—blind-folded, or with eyes closed?

Thread the Needle

Can you balance on one knee and thread a needle?

Kick the Ball

Try tossing up a basketball so that it lands behind you, kick it with feet.

Dog Jump

Can you jump over a stick held in the hands, or through your clasped hands?

Pick Up Chair

Make a toe line 2 feet from wall, with a chair between. Lean forward, put head against the wall, pick up chair, and recover your balance.

Water Toter

Carry a glass or pan full of water across the room or for several paces, without spilling any.

Pick Up Magazine

Stand on one foot, hold other behind, lean forward, and pick up a magazine in teeth. (It could be the magazine of the organization.)

Dropping Marbles

Hold them waist high, see who can drop the most into a bottle or small can.

Jump Your Toe

Holding toes of either foot in the hand, can you jump the free foot over the held one without letting go?

Pulling Out the Napkin

With a bottle on a napkin on the table, can you take the napkin from under the bottle without touching bottle or knocking it over? Rap the table hard enough to bounce bottle up, gradually pulling out the napkin each time?

Salt Shaker Standing on Side

Can you make a hexagonal-shaped salt shaker stand on its side at a 45 degree angle? This is possible by pouring a small pile of salt on the table and working the shaker, set at a 45 degree angle, down until it is about one salt grain of thickness from the table. It may take several tries, but it definitely can be done.

Putting Coin into Cup

There is a coin in front of a cup standing on a table. Can you put the coin in the cup without touching the coin? Yes, by striking the table underneath the coin, thus making the coin land in the cup.

Coin Catch

Put several coins on your elbow, held out shoulder high with palm down. Try to drop coins off the elbow and catch them in the same hand. To make it harder, spread them out on the elbow.

Balloon Blow

With the second hand of a watch, see who can keep a balloon (or feather) in the air the longest.

Kneel, and Lift Chair

Can you kneel on your right knee at the side of a chair, take the lower end of back leg in your right hand and lift the chair from the floor? (Make these "left" if left-handed.)

Putting Cork into Bottle

With a bottle on the floor, cork sitting loosely in place, stand on one foot and try to hop, pushing down the cork into bottle with that same foot. (The foot bearing your weight is the one to push in the cork.)

Croquet First

With the second hand of a watch, see who can make the regular rounds of a croquet court in the least time.

Miniature Golf, Fast

Do the same with a miniature golf course laid out, with small balls or golf balls, hockey sticks for golf sticks. The winner completes in shortest time.

Sticky Glass

Cup your palm over a full glass of water, then suddenly straighten out your fingers. The glass will adhere to the palm.

Curvy Blow

Put a lighted candle behind a bottle. Blow on the other side of the bottle and put the light out.

Making Egg Stand on End

You can make a hard-boiled egg stand in an upright position on a plate by making small horizontal circles with the plate.

Figure Magic

Have people take any even number, multiply it by 3, divide that by 2, multiply by 3. To give them the answer, ask how many times 9 will go into it, double what they give you, and you have the answer!

Reverse Actions

Can you obey instructions in reverse, or give wrong answers. This is fun to try on a group.

Eleven Matches Make Nine

Who can place 6 matches, side by side, add 5 more and make 9? You spell out, "NINE."

Blindfold Drawing

While blindfolded, can you draw a picture of a girl on the blackboard?

Singing Backward

Who can sing "America, the Beautiful," backward? (Turn your back to the audience and sing.)

Touching a Book

Can you touch a book outside and inside without opening it? (Yes, outdoors and indoors!)

Palm Read in Five Seconds

After giving this a build-up, put a drop of mercurochrome or a red chalk mark in the middle of the person's hand.

Jump a Pencil

Can you put a pencil on the floor, stand with toes almost touching it, toes grasped in hands, and jump over it?

Raise the Broom

Try taking a broom in your right hand (left if you are left-handed) and from the far end, work it up until you have the "broom end."

Turn the Glass

With your right elbow at your side, palm up, put a full glass of water on your hand; see if you can swing hand around underneath armpit and complete the turn without spilling water.

Coin Turn Trick

Can you put a coin on your little finger and do the same thing, without dropping the coin?

Hand Slap

One player has hands extended, palms up. The other has his hands extended, palms down toward those of first player. The "palms up" player takes the aggressive, trying to slap the backs of the hands of his opponent without warning. The opponent, of course, tries to get his hands out of the way. Reverse after a while.

Coin Grab

One person has a coin in his palm with hand open. He is to try to close palm and keep coin, while the other, who starts with his hand, palm down, about 6 inches above, tries to grab the coin. By making a quick "slapping motion," thus forcing coin to jump, he will get it nearly every time.

Pull Them Apart

Can you pull apart the hands of a player who has his elbows out to his sides, tips of middle fingers touching at his chest?

Bull Ring

Name it what you like, but draw a circle a few feet in diameter, and see if you can pull your opponent into the ring, he (the bull) resisting.

Ball Wrestle

One person holds a volleyball or basketball or other ball of that size. The other tries to wrest it from him. May be timed.

Wrist Wrestle

Two players interlace fingers. The object is to force your opponent to his knees.

Back Bend

Place a crumpled piece of paper about 25 to 30 inches behind your heels. Kneel on both knees, arms on chest, and see if you can lean over backward and get the paper (or handkerchief) in your teeth.

Tying the Calf

Two players, with shoes off, have ropes, and in two minutes or less are trying at the same time to tie up opponent's ankles but to keep from being tied. It's rough!

Buzz

Three players stand side by side, firmly braced with wide stance, the middle one with hat on. Each outside player has his outside hand to his face, fingers directed toward center player, who will later try to slap those fingers. The inside arm of each player is free. The center one starts buzzing, first one and then the other, tantalizing. Finally he strikes— by slapping the hand of one of the players (near his face). This player may then (and not before) try to knock the hat off the center one. If so, he goes to center.

Some Self-Testing Actions[1]

Take ten steps forward on a straight line.

Jump into air and clap feet together once.

[1] From Harry D. Edgren, George Williams College, Chicago, Ill.

Lie flat on floor, arms folded, and come up to sitting position.

Arms folded behind back, kneel on both knees and get up without losing balance.

Push up three times.

Squat position, hands crossed in front of body, jump to a stride with hands horizontal sideward.

Make a full pirouette to left.

Jump into air and clap feet together twice.

Stand on right foot, grasp left foot behind right knee, bend and touch left knee to the floor, and stand up without losing balance.

Hold toes of either foot in opposite hand, jump up with free foot over foot that is held, without letting it go.

Jump into air and slap both heels behind your back with your hands.

Stand and kick the right foot shoulder high.

Stand on left foot, bend forward, and place both hands on the floor, raise right leg, stretch it back, touch head to floor, and return to standing position.

Stand with both feet together, bend down, hands between legs around outside of ankles, and hold fingers together in front of ankles for five seconds.

Make full pirouette to the right.

Kneel on both knees, sit down, and get up without unfolding arms.

Stand on left foot, hold bottom of right foot against inside of left knee for ten seconds, eyes closed.

Take frog stand position.

Stand on left foot, sit down on left heel, and stand up again.

Push away from the wall.

Jump and reach, make highest mark.

FORFEITS AND INITIATION STUNTS

Several of those already given would be suitable for forfeits and initiations, especially for boys. Here are some other suggestions:

1. Tongue twisters. (Make them read these three times.)
   Six gray geese on green grass grazing.
   Six thick thistle sticks.
   Round and round the rugged rock the ragged rascal ran.
   Copper coffee pot.
   Ziggy Jazinski.
2. Sing a song (perhaps a lullaby).
3. Yawn until somebody in the group yawns, too.
4. Read or say something funny without laughing.
5. Put your hand where the other hand can't reach it (on the elbow).
6. Say a number of complimentary things about yourself.
7. With one hand, move a number of beans one by one from one dish to another. (Between two, this could be a race.)
8. Fill a glass with water, using a thimble (could be a race).
9. Put a number of marbles in a milk bottle, with a fork.
10. Pile up twelve tin cans without letting them fall.

The Handbook of Skits and Stunts, by Helen and Larry Eisenberg, is the forerunner volume to *Fun with Skits, Stunts, and Stories,* with no duplication of content. Contains one-person stunts, "quickies," narrator stunts, physical feats and tricks, stunts from other lands, plus "how-to-helps." (Association Press, 291 Broadway, New York 7, N. Y., 254 pages.)

Drama Clubs, Step by Step, by Charles F. Wells, contains skits and stunts, plus help for organizing a drama club for more serious productions. (Walter H. Baker Company, 569 Boylston Street, Boston 16, Massachusetts.)

Handy Stunts, by Lynn Rohrbough, is filled with skit and stunt suggestions. (Co-operative Recreation Services, Delaware, Ohio, 48 pages.)

Hilarious Stunts, by Harry Githens, is an older collection with several usable stunts. (Eldridge Publishing Company, Franklin, Ohio, 131 pages.)

Conscience on Stage, by Harold Ehrensperger, represents a fine and unusually creative approach to drama. (Abingdon-Cokesbury Press, Nashville, Tennessee.)

357 Songs We Love to Sing is packed with familiar songs. Gives full piano accompaniments. (Hall-McCreary, 434 South Wabash Avenue, Chicago, Illinois.)

Skits Hits and *The End of Your Stunt Hunt,* by Helen and Larry Eisenberg, each contain several stunts of the general nature of those in this book. (Fun Books, 5847 Gregory, Hollywood, California, 64 and 48 pages, respectively.)

How to Help Folks Have Fun, by Helen and Larry Eisenberg, is a compilation of hundreds of fun ideas, with stunts included. (Association Press, 291 Broadway, New York 7, N. Y., 64 pages.)

INDEX

If used with the Table of Contents on page 7, this alphabetical index will serve fully as a "use index." These skits, stunts and stories, with few exceptions, have been selected for universal use with teen and adult groups of either sex or both sexes. They are equally suitable for use in homes, churches, community centers, clubs and social centers, small dining rooms, large banquet halls, and camps, either indoors or out. All are readily adaptable for any special occasion.